1

Calm
Instead of Clamor

How to Control the Natural Gift of Fear

By

J. Traveler Pelton, LISW-S

POTPOURRI
PUBLISHING

copyright © 2020
Potpourri Publishing, Limited
Mt. Vernon, OH 43050

COPYRIGHT

ligularia

Dedication

First, to my God and Creator, Savior and Guide, who gives us dreams and tasks, who gifts us with imagination and who breathes life into our dreams.

I dedicate with love to all those who have been to the shadowy edge of life, looked over and decided to come back and try again. I've been there, I came back. May you keep the warmth and wealth of love in your hearts always. Love is what keeps us whole.

I dedicate it to my ancestors who walked the Red Road before me. Someday we will all walk the Skylands together. Until then our hearts beat with the drum of unity and peace.

May God grant us the courage to live with whatever life sends us and overcome trials always with His peace.

Finally, to my readers, because a story isn't a story until someone else hears it; it is simply a phantasm, a dream in the maker's head. You make it live when you read it and for just a few brief moments, our imaginations combine and that's when magic is still alive...

Other Books by Traveler Pelton

Spiritual Works
- God Wanted to Write a Bestseller
- Big God, Little Me
- Lenten Stories for God's Little Children
- Natural Morning
- Ninety Days to The God Habit
- Tales for Advent and Christmas
- His Path Is Mine
- Calm Instead of Clamor

Christian Literary Science Fiction

The First Oberllyn Family Trilogy: The Past
- The Oberllyn's Overland: 1855-1862
- Terrorists, Traitors and Spies 1900-1990
- Rebooting the Oberllyn's 2015-2020

The Second Oberllyn Family Trilogy: The Present
- The Infant Conspiracy
- Kai Dante's Stratagem
- The Obligation of Being Oberllyn

The Third Oberllyn Family Trilogy: The Future
- To Protect One's Own
- The Importance of Family Ties
- Kith and Kin, Together Again

The Fiber Mavens Mystery Series
- Quilting Can be Criminal
- Criminally Quilted

Family History
- Journey to Springhaven

Other Authors Associated with Potpourri Publishing

In Collaboration with T. Bear Pelton:
- Clan Falconer's War
- The Rise of the Rebellion
- Changeling's Clan
- Forged in Water and Fire

Lynette Spencer of Write Useful
- Sewing on a Budget
- Vegetarian Cooking on a Budget

Dan Pelton
The Majestic Spectrum of God's Love

Table of Contents

Preface

Welcome to your latest journey with me. I am honored you have joined me, as you may have done in my previous books (*Ninety Days to the God Habit, Natural Morning, Big God, Little Me*, etc.). We walk this path for a short time and I hope you gain the knowledge and the peace you need in our trying world from our little walk together. It is my belief you are not reading this without a reason: I believe God works in His own ways and own time and this book is in your hands because He wants it there.

This book centers on fear, what it is, what it does to you, and how to control the anxiety it causes within you. My aim is to assist you in trying to locate a place of peace within yourself that will help you to walk in serenity to a better time. It's time to gain control of your own panic, your own loneliness, and your own fears. It's time to use the energy from those fears to give you the power to move on and control what you can and leave the rest to God. As a Christian counselor, I spend my office days working with people of all ages and walks of life. I have seen a disturbing trend of late and that trend is what prompted me to ask you to come and walk a little way with this old counselor; I hope you find the walk worthwhile.

Today's prevalent emotion among those I encounter appears to be fear: fear of the pandemic, fear of war, loneliness, losing their job, going bankrupt, losing their home, losing their mate, their health, being non-essential or irrelevant, growing old, being weak or simply "at-risk" or out and out dying. The recent events in our world in dealing with the Covid-19 pandemic have only seemed to exacerbate our fears. For most of us, the inner fears we have been hoarding in our hearts like hidden treasures have been pretty well under control; we put on a good face, we're functional, we go to work, to church, to school, home and do our chores, go to bed and then don't sleep. Our mind whirls with what we have to get done when we get up the next day, or what bill gets paid this week, or whether our kids are going to be all right. We hold it together with social supports that we clung to, job, church, friends, shopping, parks; all the vestiges of civilization. We are the walking desperate, smiling, cordial, scared spitless.

It was hard, we held it together, and then the leaders of many states and the Federal government started doing daily on-air conferences to bring us up to date on the latest deaths and spread and dangers out there which just seems to exacerbate our fear. They mean well; they want to avoid panic, in reality, it feeds the fear. Just as we thought it couldn't get worse, to protect us our government put out mandatory stay at home orders and suddenly, the job was gone that distracted us and enabled us to feel like we were competent and able to care for ourselves, the ones who were able to work found themselves in essential but risky jobs, the school that watched and taught our kids was closed, leaving us to try and teach at home with packets or loaned tablets; the daycare closed down; the grandparents were high risk so couldn't help; boredom became epidemic. The church went online and we no longer can gain comfort from the closeness of others of like belief. Even the counselors we go to try and make some sense of it all talk to us online or by phone and not in person as if even humanity itself is contagious. When we start getting psychosomatic symptoms, we call our doctors only to find our doctors will see us only using teletherapy, there is not even the comfort of human touch when being examined. Our skin is hungry. We are suddenly hedgehogs trying to be friendly; edging closer but not within six feet; prickly and fearful, rolled up into our own little balls of thorns. One by one, our supports are being kicked out from under us, and we dangle, hanging, gasping, not knowing whether there is rescue out there, or simply a long, painful collapse towards oblivion.

We have nightmares that wake us up shaking. Those of us who have children worry now that they won't get a good education because they have all these little packets to fill out or do online instead of regular classes, yet sending them to school in light of the possibility of severe illness or death is also unthinkable. My colleagues who have to try and teach college courses online to students shake their heads, one chemistry professor says he's teaching kitchen chemistry now, he isn't able to be present to explain the intricacies of the subject. The students who are to complete the semester they've paid for and get something memorable out of the subject find it impossible to bounce ideas off each other, or face to face ask the professor what something means; their frustration is notable. Many are finding that the day to day reactions and intercommunication with the minds of others is what made learning good, it caused them to think, it got the creative ideas linking up and they felt and knew the information was settling into their minds where it could be accessed later when needed. It was deep learning; it wasn't shallow, learning only to get this next quiz done. It made their worldview, their vocabulary, adjust to new thoughts, it deepened and changed them into their profession-to-be. I have spoken to people who are frantic because their pre-med or pre-law students can't get the education they need to pass the GRE or the MCAT or the LSAT entrance tests, and all their hard work trying to get through undergrad school is for nothing

15

since the preparation time they need is not happening. They aren't getting their knives sharpened, as my old grandpa used to say, they aren't being honed for life.

Those of us who work in the health field try our best to stay safe: with N95 masks all but unavailable, hand sanitizer being made at home and carried to work; gloves in short supply, blood in short supply because people aren't going out to give blood, the lack of basic equipment like ventilators. Those of us in the behavioral health field are seeing more stressed, frightened, and almost suicidal people; sometimes when a person comes into the office, they carry their fear with them on their shoulders and you can see it in their body language. Their shoulders droop, their smile is tentative, they have lost their confidence; their views are pessimistic. They reach out to shake hands and yank their hands back remembering we can't touch. Daily broadcasts on TV to keep us all up to date are almost obsessively watched; we take hints on what the next thing is we have to buy frantically for fear we will not have enough, be it toilet paper or hand sanitizer, vitamin C or lemons.

Lemons?

The other day, I had a woman come into my office frustrated about lemons. She had read online that lemons will help protect you from the COVID-19 virus and the flu virus and SARS and any other virus, all you had to do was slice them into a cup and fill it with hot water and drink it like tea. Well and good, so she went out and bought a bag of lemons, took them home, and remembered she was allergic to lemons! She wanted me to tell her what to do. She was so anxious she had lost the ability to process information. She had twenty lemons and they gave her hives. We all need to calm down but it seems we can all fall for the hype.

We listen, we watch the social media build-up our premonitions of danger, we stay home to try and do our part, we only go out on essential trips and we allow ourselves to dwell on the present and not see a future anymore. We actually start believing the conspiracy people. It's as if mass hysteria is becoming the norm. We were never, never supposed to live this way.

The human psyche was not built to live as hermits. I will tell you upfront that this book was written from a Christian perspective, but much of it is taken from research done in the ways to control anxiety and fear, things I teach people in my office, and yes, sometimes now by phone. There are simple things that can be done to lift your outlook and make the present more bearable, to give you hope; to stop the panic.

I was reading the scriptures the other day and came across this verse I hadn't noticed before, or if I had, hadn't applied to myself. It's from the prophet Isaiah, speaking to his people as they were contemplating yet another war brought on by their disobedience.

"Come, my people, enter your chambers, and shut your doors behind you; Hide yourself, as it were, for a little moment, Until the indignation (also translated His wrath) is past." *Isaiah 26:20*

The people of Israel were being told to wait it out; to go into self-quarantine until it was over. God didn't say worry; he didn't say fret, he didn't say shake in your boots; he said hideaway. In other words, build yourself an ark of safety in your home and wait patiently for Him to work out the mess. Those who obeyed would be safe. Those who didn't would not be safe. As in the days of the Passover in the time of Moses, the people were to shelter inside their houses, waiting for the passing of the angel of death, eating a special meal to allow them to have strength for the journey to a new and strange and better place, a place of freedom. We are to follow that idea, claim this promise that it will pass and go on.

So, as we begin another journey, one back to sanity and stability and security and health, we'll start simply with some ideas and suggestions that have been found by research to actually be useful; simple changes you can do right now. You don't have to wait to read the entire book: start in part one of chapter one and practice the simple skills. They help. In addition, I have written a companion book that has short devotionals for each day if you want to add those to your regime during the day to take your mind away from the troubles on this old earth and into another realm. It's called *Calm My Clamor.*

Here begins your trip from fear to tranquility. It's not meant to change the world, it's made to change us, one at a time, to work through our fears and set them aside, to learn to trust that all this shall pass in its own good time. We need to hunker down until it's over. I hope you enjoy the journey and learn to walk this path with confidence.

Chapter 1-A:
Calming Breaths

Being at heart a systematic and efficient person, I want to begin our journey with a sensible approach you can use right now in the next fifteen minutes to start the calming of your mind. I want you to silence those screeching voices in your head that are making you anxious and convincing you that this pandemic is going to be like the Black Death of the Middle ages. The fears keep you from resting, they prevent you from thinking things through, causing you to make bad choices. (Remember the lady with the bag of lemons? How about people thinking they actually need 96 rolls of toilet paper? Are you convinced you can't teach your kids math? Someone told you coronavirus is a Chinese plot to bring down the country? You are not being rational. You're panicking.) You would like to shut that siren in your head off as well, I think, but don't know where your off switch is located. The next couple of chapters help you locate your switch and turn it off, or at least way down. There is a way to calm down and give you enough respite that you can take in new ideas once more, process them reasonably, and get on with your life with a new, quieter, and firmer perspective. After we have gone through beginning suggestions to start within Chapter One, we'll explain what fear is and why it affects us as it does, why we are anxious and why we panic so easily. For now, though, let's do some practical things to start us on this journey.

There will be more scattered throughout this book, but these first ones are essential to master. They cost nothing but practice time. With everyone in their homes, we have practice time available. The really good thing about all this is that you can use these all the rest of your life whenever things get out of hand or out of control or overwhelming. They work so much better if you have them firmly in mind. Ideally, we should have been taught these before we entered kindergarten, we all need these skills.

This section of the book contains seven beginner tools to start with: some very simple things to do to begin your journey more comfortable. You need to master them to make later use of them when you are anxious. The first exercise is very simple. I need to teach you to breathe.

I know, you think we all want to keep breathing and that's today's predominant problem; the present pandemic makes breathing hard to do and stops it completely in 2% of those who catch Covid-19, but I mean a different kind of breathing. I call it calming breathing. For it, you need a comfortable place free of most distractions and you need the air around you. If you want very quiet environmental music in your background, that's fine. Turn off the phone, the TV, the video games. It has to be quiet, like go to bed quiet. Floors are seldom comfortable enough for this, but you can lie on the floor if you want.

Find a comfortable chair, couch, or bed. Sit or lie in a relaxed position, shoulders not hunched up, hands loose, legs stretched out. Take a second to snuggle into a very relaxed position. Close your eyes. Take a big breath in through your nose, hold it, out through your mouth, slowly.

Count to yourself, breathe in, one, two, three, out as you blow it all out, one, two, three. Each time, feel the air go in through your nose, recognize that your body is heavy, that your belly seems to pump way up and then down, your head feels a little light. Do this five times, each time a little slower. Let's go over that again.

Breathe in through your nose, count 1, 2 out through your mouth count 1,2.

Breathe in, one, two, three, hold onto it, one, two, breathe out one, two, three.

Breathe in one, two, three, hold it, one two three, blow out one, two, three; feel the air in your lungs, feel the quiet in your mind as you concentrate on breathing and counting to yourself

Breathe in one, two, three, hold it in one, two, three, four - you'll feel just a little tension as you hold it in for a count of four, blow out one, two, three-you'll feel almost a feeling of release

Final breath in this sequence, in one, two, three hold it, one, two, three, four, five, push it all out; one, two, three.

Open your eyes. Roll your shoulders back and quietly get up (Or if doing this before bed, turn to another position and snuggle down to sleep. You need to do this exercise twice a day to start, once before you get out of bed in the morning, once before you go to bed; therefore, the best place to practice at first is bed. Your bed should trigger you to think of being warm and relaxed.

After you have practiced this in bed in the morning and night for five days and feel pretty confident in it, add a midday session. The midday session is where you will add more exercises to do.

For the first few days, get your body used to the idea that when we breathe like this, we are not worrying, we're getting ready to rest. We are sending your brain and body the signal that things are peaceful at the day start and the tail end of the day. Nothing to be worried about. Your body will learn that when you breathe like this, it needs to relax.

You are training your mind.

Have you ever considered that you need to train your mind? It shouldn't be allowed to toddle around by itself getting into mischief and making bad choices. You need to direct it. (More is coming on that later!)

Now, some people are so weary they fall asleep, or they doze off during the first few times they do this and that's OK. It shows just how tired you were. You've been too hard on yourself.

When you wake up, or when you simply open your eyes to start the day or go on to the next exercise, your brain will have been given a boost of oxygen, and you'll feel a little less like dashing around frantically. Every day, you need to practice this kind of breathing twice a day: when you wake in the morning before you get out of bed, to energize your brain, and at night as you lay down to go to sleep, to relax. It needs to become a habit to breathe calmly twice a day, sort of oasis in the stress of life, 3 minutes in the morning and evening you give yourself.

You are worth 6 minutes a day, right?

Once you have mastered calming breathing, it's time to go to the second quick exercise.

Chapter 1-B
Relaxing It All

List of needs

YOU-- the most important tool

A timer of some sort that will time 3 minutes and ring or beep or screech-the exact tonality doesn't matter; it has to get your attention

A reward that has value to you-something very simply you enjoy but is not costly or hard to find

Got it all assembled? Let's begin.

For the second exercise, using your breathing as a backdrop, you will need a timer-be it on your watch or a kitchen timer or a second hand on a clock. It needs to be able to ding loud enough to alert you in three minutes. You will also need a reward: I don't care if it's a chocolate Easter egg or a shiny apple or a walk outside in the sunlight or a spritz of your favorite perfume (my personal choice is to take a walk until I find something blooming and sniff it, in winter, a spritz of my favorite perfume is a close second.). It has to be something tangible, something physical that will involve at least one of your senses and something that you enjoy normally. It needs to be familiar. It needs to **not** be alcohol, drugs, or something that will fog your brain. We want to clear your mind, not anesthetize it. Drugging a mind never lasts for long and when you come back from the high or the drunk you feel worse than when you started.

The first thing to do when you feel overwhelmed or fearful is to allow yourself to recognize how you feel, not deny it or mush it down inside where it can bubble and boil and hurt you. Recognize the feeling for what it is, a feeling, nothing more. It can be adjusted as you like and as you choose. You are in control of your mind. It's not as if your brain was independent of you; breathe deep a couple of times, let it know you're relaxing, and then follow these instructions.

Sit down somewhere you are comfortable. This exercise is not for in bed. Set your timer for three minutes. Lean back and close your eyes. Breathe in through your nose and blow out through your mouth, do it again and notice how it feels to breathe in deeply and then blow it out slowly. On the third breath in, tell yourself something like this:

*"I really don't like how I feel, but it is how I feel. I am angry/fearful/upset/overwhelmed (whatever fits) but that is ok. It's how I feel now, not how I am going to stay. All things change. I will too. The most used phrase in the Bible is Fear Not! God knew we get scared easy and I'm no different than anyone else. All of this will pass. I can handle what is going on. I am not alone, even with social distancing. There is a world all around me, from birds in the park to people walking by, from my family and my friends and most of all God and His Spirit. I am never truly alone. I am a part of this world He made. While physically there may be no one here (*or there may feel like too many if all the kids are home*) I am like an oasis of calm. I breathe in, I breathe out and I feel the tension leave me."*

Continue to breathe in, out, slower each time, for three minutes, and remembering you are not alone. Consider thoughts like the ones I wrote above-they aren't for memorizing, they're here as an example of what to think about. Some people find it helpful to record the above little speech to yourself and personalize it, then as they relax, they play it and listen and absorb the words. If that helps, fine, do it. The important thing is to not think about finances or kids' grades or where you're going to get supplies. Think only of being in control, of being able, capable, and forgiving of yourself.

When your timer alerts you, open your eyes, stretch, and go take your reward. Smell something like a flower, or eat a small treat-3 M&M's or a candy kiss, or a piece of fruit. Pet your dog or cat and think of how smooth their fur feels. Or if you're a spinner like I am, go pet some roving; angora and merino are both nice to your fingers. Your reward has to be sensual, tactile, rewarding. Enjoy it for a few minutes and get on with your day. You need to do this little exercise each day at least once. Your body will learn to relax, and with that relaxation, comes a better response to life's problems. It really is a very simple exercise.

Does any of this sound familiar to those who have taken psychology in high school? Does it sound a little like you are treating your body like Pavlov's dog, learning a response? Exactly - and the strange thing is, it really works for people, too. You are taking control of your body and teaching it to respond as you want it to whatever trigger comes along. In this second exercise, you are showing it that with relaxation comes reward-you successfully do your exercise and it gets a Hershey's kiss(taste) or a nice smell(a spritz of a favorite odor) or some time outside looking at flowers(sight), or you pet your cat (touch)-whatever is a simple reward to the senses, use it to train your mind.

Chapter 1-C
RAK - Your Secret Weapon

Our next exercise, number three, is to practice a Random Act of Kindness each day. Somewhere in the day, call your mother. I am not kidding. Or call someone else who is also shut in; you parents, relatives, friends-one call a day to someone else; it lifts your spirit. It lifts theirs. It shows you are concerned about them. Don't text, call. You need to hear a human voice. The sound of their voice is a reward to you, and you to them.

In fact, I suggest to my clients they make a phone list of as many family and friends as they have, be sure there is a phone number by each name and each day, go down the list and call one. Make it at a specific time of day, every day. Hearing other people's voices, people you know helps your own sense of grounding.

Does this sound too simple? There is sound science behind it. Research has shown that people who step out of their own comfort zone to do something for someone else actually allow their body to release oxytocin-sometimes called the love hormone. Here are just a few quotes from research being done-there are literally thousands:

"According to research done at Emory University, when you do something kind for someone else, your brain's pleasure centers are activated, as if you had been the recipient of the kind deed. This phenomenon is called "the Helper's high." (retrieved from http://www.ccnl.emory.edu/Publicity/MSNBC.HTM)

"Committing acts of kindness lowers blood pressure. According to Dr. David R. Hamilton, acts of kindness create emotional warmth, which releases a hormone known as oxytocin. Oxytocin causes the release of a chemical called nitric oxide, which dilates the blood vessels. This reduces blood pressure and, therefore, oxytocin is known as a "cardioprotective" hormone. It protects the heart by lowering blood pressure. (retrieved from https://drdavidhamilton.com/the-5-side-effects-of-kindness/)"

"Stephen Post of Case Western Reserve University School of Medicine found that when we give of ourselves, everything from life satisfaction to self-realization and physical health is significantly improved. Mortality is delayed, depression is reduced and well-being and good fortune are increased. Dr. Stephen Post, Ph.D. bioethics professor, Case Western Reserve University School of Medicine (retrieved from https://www.researchgate.net/publication/7840821_Altruis m_Happiness_and_Health_It's_Good_to_Be_Good)"

"The positive effects of kindness are experienced in the brain of everyone who witnessed the act, improving their mood and making them significantly more likely to "pay it forward." This means one good deed in a crowded area can create a domino effect and improve the day of dozens of people! Jamil Zaki, Assistant Professor of Psychology at Stanford University for Scientific American, July 26, 2016"

"Perpetually kind people have 23% less cortisol (the stress hormone) and age slower than the average population!" Integrative Psychological and Behavioral Science, 1998 (retrieved from https://www.ncbi.nlm.nih.gov/pubmed/9737736)"

I could quote dozens more-but the simple fact is that doing something kind for someone else each day will make you stronger, happier, and less anxious. The reason I chose a simple phone call as a place to start is that at the time of this writing, we are all in a mandatory shelter at home situation due to the Covid-19 virus. You can't go help someone cross the street or even be within six feet of anyone, but you have a phone, I'm guessing, and you know someone who would benefit from a call just to see how they're getting on.

Or perhaps you can make masks for people. I know one person who made over the course of three days, over a hundred cotton face masks, then, putting one on herself, dropped all the rest off at the local fire department for them to hand out to others. Still, another found that the world's largest department store chain, Walmart, had required their workers to wear masks, they had to be a solid color, and she realized that many of them couldn't sew. She and two others talked it over online and they made over fifty masks, went to the office at the local store, and donated them to be given to any worker who had a need.

I know personally of one woman who takes fifteen minutes every morning to write a short note, acknowledging her gratitude to someone, be it a friend, a relative, and lately she has been putting all the local agencies on her list to get notes. The fire department, the police, the sheriff, the local hospital, each floor and department get a separate note. She says the walk to the mailbox to drop off her notes makes her feel good each day.

One man I know raises chickens and gifts those in his neighborhood who may be struggling financially with fresh eggs. Still another person looks up a few funny memes each day and sends them to specific people who he thinks might need cheered up with a little note to them online. There are dozens of ways to be kind.

Think about it; find someone to be kind to each day. You will be surprised at how good it makes you feel.

Chapter 1-D
Taking a Mental Vacation

This idea has a tendency to make some folks uncomfortable for a number of reasons.

I am not describing day-dreaming, wool-gathering, spacing out. Neither am I suggesting you imagine yourself to a better life, or think hard about it so that you can get it, expecting to make yourself into some sort of genie. Nor am I trying to teach you a New Age religious vision quest.

I am talking about using your own memories, your own imagination to control fear long enough for you to get your wits about you and stop the hormones rapidly coursing everywhere in your body and making your feel helpless and overwhelmed. I am talking about returning control to your conscious mind from your subconscious mind.

It is done in one of two ways: the first I find simpler. The second takes a bit more work, but is used to good effect by thousands of people. Let's do the first one to start.

I want you to look back into your own memories, your own life and find a time you felt truly happy, in control, relaxed, at ease. It can be a holiday as a child, or your wedding, the birth of your first child, the first time you rode a merry-go-round. It can be the day you got that promotion at work. It can be graduating, or Christmas or grandma's house on Thanksgiving. I had one teen boy who told me it was the feeling he got from making a basket in a good game, or hitting the ball out of the park. Another person told me what her college major was going to be and finding out her folks approved of it, as she thought they might not. Still another person told me the first leading role she got in her theater troop was her biggest thrill to date. It has to be a good memory that is yours.

Once you have that memory, I want you to compress it down to a snapshot in your head, or a short video. Look at it from different angles, remember how you felt, what it smelled like, if it's something physical, what it tactilely seemed to be when touched. It has to fill your senses in your head. So, if it's a Christmas memory, who was there, what did the tree smell like, did someone touch you, was it a special toy you wanted, was it something you ate that was just so good-describe it with your mind to yourself. Pretend you are a photographer trying to get the best focused picture you can. When you have it firmly in mind, stop. Put it aside and start your breathing sequence, in, out, relax your muscles and then put yourself back into the picture, carefully breathing slower, deeper, and relax. When you have completed your 5 breaths, stop the picture and pull back. The entire exercise takes 5 breaths, that's all, but if you practice with persistence, when feelings of dread, fear, anxiety start welling up, you can take a deep breath and take yourself out of the situation and back to that happy memory.

It takes your brain about thirty seconds to reset and stop making the alarm chemicals caused by your false perception of danger. In the 45 seconds this exercise takes, you have told your body there is nothing wrong, you are calm, and you need to think. Your frontal lobe (your conscious mind) kicks back in, and you are back again, calm, relaxed and able to think clearly.

I have used this myself when in uncomfortable situations, for instance, when I am on the stand as a witness and the opposing counsel is trying to discredit me as a witness and is hammering on something that actual may not even have anything to do with the case, trying to get me rattled. I slow things down by not answering his questions until after I have taken one deep breath. If he gets really obnoxious, I do it twice and flash back to my childhood, when my dad brought us home our first pony, a little black horse named Midnight. I smile at the lawyer, and ask him to repeat his question so I am sure I answer it correctly. When they try to speed up, I slow down. At any rate, you slow the racing down too, by refusing to allow it to take over.

There are some people who really, because of the chaos and hurt in their lives, have no happy memories they can recall. They were neglected as children, abused as adults and trying to find something cheerful takes them too much mental energy they don't have right now. For them, I use the second form of mental vacation. We make a memory.

I ask them to imagine the sort of natural spot they would like to visit, be it ocean, mountains, forest, a cabin on the lake, whatever. Once they have chosen, then we look into constructing that place. Let's use ocean as an example.

Imagine you are walking along the edge of the sea, the place where the water comes up often enough it has made the sand firm. Imagine there is no one there but you and the shorebirds; it's early morning, the tide has gone out, and the shorebirds are running around picking up bits here and there on their spindly legs. There are gulls calling overhead, and here and there, tiny crabs scurry to find shelter in clumps of seaweed. You look out over the waves a moment: the rising sun makes a golden pathway across the sea and far out there are some early sailboats floating. The waves rush up just enough to cover your feet and as they draw back, you hear the birds, you hear the swishing of the waves as they come up to play tag with you. The air smells like salt and fresh air. Looking far down the beach, you see another person out and they seem to be picking up shells. You decide you'd do that awhile and you feel inside you pockets and find you have a Ziploc bag of crumbs. You spend a moment tossing them to the chore birds and then look for shells to fill you bag. You walk peacefully and you feel refreshed.

Now, whatever you construct for your good memory, make it as realistic as you can. If you need to watch a couple videos of the sea, or even visit the ocean yourself to get a better feel, then do it. Then make a snapshot, the best parts.

Once your mind gets used to the idea that this is your relaxation picture, and there's no danger, anytime something difficult comes up, you can take a breath and be back on vacation for thirty seconds. Studies have shown that people who use this technique can lower their blood pressure by several points, just be relaxing in a memory.

So, your assignment from this section of chapter 1 is to remember a memory. You'd not want to forget it anyway, right? Now is the time to make it clear as crystal in your head. When you practice your breathing and relaxing each day, add your memory to it.

Chapter 1-E
Counting Your Blessings Isn't Just for Old Folks!

I heard a young, angry person scoff one day when I mentioned this idea of being grateful that the idea of counting good things was something people did a long time ago; it's just for old folks! He was wrong, as young folks with strong opinions are apt to be sometimes.

Our fourth practical exercise is to simply write down all the good things in your life. The fact that you are healthy enough to write something down is a start! List the things you love, your blessings as those of us old-fashioned folks like to say.

From the dog barking next door to the birds in the trees, to the fact you are alive to see another day, to the children driving you nuts; you can write down short lists, ten or so on each list, multiple lists like a game. Then post those lists where you will see them during the day; on the fridge door, on the bathroom mirror, on the bedside stand. Use your imagination and figure out where the thought of the good things in your life will be helpful to you.

One client wrote her lists on 3 x 5 cards she kept in her pocket and pulled out when she was at work as a nurse. She'd laminated them so she could wipe them off as needed. She'd carry them in one of the many pockets on her scrubs. When she felt down, she would pull out one card of 5 blessings, study it and stick it back. No one thought anything about it because nurses are always carrying things around in their pockets to take notes on. She would whip it out, read the first two or three, and get back to work. It helped her to visualize that there was still good in the world even if someone just threw up on her or fell out of bed or won't stop ringing their call light for silly things or someone was difficult to care for; there is always good somewhere.

Another person told me they organized their blessings into groups of three, and taped them inside kitchen cabinets, a different list in each cabinet or drawer so whenever he opened the cabinet for anything, there was a blessing list to glimpse through.

Put the list where it's useful and easy for you to see. So, you may ask at this point, "Where do I start?"

I always tell people to start with their own basic needs. Be thankful for your health, your home, your job, your family, and your friends. List them in separate columns or on separate cards. Under each basic thing, list three things about it that are good.

For instance, my list under health includes, "I am still in remission from cancer after 15 years. I have the ability to take care of myself. I am not ill and neither is anyone in my family."

Under my home, I have written, "I am glad I have a home. I am glad it's paid for and I don't have to worry about losing it in uncertain times. I am thankful it has electricity and gas and phone service. I am pleased there is a fence to keep my animals out of my neighbor's yards. I am thankful for my neighbors, although we can't do much together right now. I am thankful that I have clothes suitable for any time of year and weather because in Ohio, let's just say the weather is variable and leave it at that. I have a car to drive that is in good shape, nothing fancy but it gets me where I need to go. I have a pantry of food and necessities. All my basic physical needs are met here on this little farm."

36

Under my job, it gets a little complicated. You see, I am semi-retired, by which I mean retired from public social service practice. I have my private behavioral health office where I go three days a week to help others.

I have my small farm where I garden, take care of my pets, and enjoy growing everything from Siamese cats to canaries to grandchildren. I have my book writing business, in which I have written 21 books in the past four years.

I help lead a small home church.

I am thankful for all my jobs. I consider them all forms of employment and enjoyment. I do not include my hobbies, like quilting and crocheting, spinning and chattering on FB with friends as jobs but they are part of this life that makes it rewarding.

Under family, I put my long-suffering husband Dan first; followed by my children and my grandchildren. I also list my church family. I list my tribal family.

On your list, you can use the same main categories or think of your own and under each category list in just a couple words what you are glad you have.

You can go broader and say you are glad the government is taking the Covid-19 menace seriously even if staying in is a mixed blessing; good as it flattens the curve; bad maybe as it makes us more anxious as continuous attention is drawn to it as a means to get folks to stay home and out of crowds.

You might list specific people or pets or things you love.

Whatever you do, make it useful for you. Put it where you can access it if you get down. Pull it out, look it over and decide if what is bothering you now disrupts or lessens any of what really matters. You would be surprised at how often that's all it takes to get you moving again towards mental peace.

Chapter 1-F
Laugh it Out

The fifth simple tool is humor. Nothing deflates fear like laughter. I have a website called travelerpelton.com. It has a humor page. I try to add new funny stories every few days and there are several dozen right now. If you are near a computer, look it up. Go to the page <u>Something Funny This Way Goes-</u> and start reading. There are so many kinds of jokes one of them is bound to help! YouTube has humor on it; find a few that always make you smile and bookmark them so when you need them, pop them up and smile.

There are a great many humor authors out there, if you have a favorite, keep a few of their books handy to read when feeling a bit down. A friend of mine got a scrapbook and each day cuts out the funniest cartoon of that day's paper and glues it into the scrapbook. When she's sad, worried, or just needs the distraction, she goes back and re-reads them. She puts a marker where she leaves off so she can go to the ones she didn't reread last time, next time.

Still another person collects humor and keeps the humor in a file she keeps in the front of her desk drawer in the office. When it's stressful, she goes to the file, reaches in and pulls out at random two or three, re-reads them, then puts them back. She says often it puts things back in perspective to smile a few moments. (She says when things are really on a tear around the office, it might take more than two or three, so she takes the file, goes to the ladies' room and in the quiet of the back corner stall, reads for ten minutes, giggles like mad, washes her face, straightens her hair and takes her file back to the office, once again the straitlaced admin assistant to the president of a large firm. I have no idea what the other ladies in the office think who come in to hear her guffawing back there, but no one has said anything to her yet.)

I remember when I worked for a public agency, many years ago, I could tell when things were coming up to a head as far as stress, and I had a file of funny sayings that I'd printed out on brightly colored 4 by 8 inch papers. I'd come in before anyone got to the office and tape them on folk's doors, funny sayings like:

You couldn't handle me even if I came with instructions.

I deserve a bonus for making it through the week without stabbing someone with a sharp object.

You people are crazy-I know…I can recognize my own kind.

Pretending I am a pleasant person all day is exhausting.

I have the ability to drive people crazy. I don't know if I was born with it or I learned it, but I am darn good at it.

If you didn't see it with your own eyes or hear it with your own ears, don't invent it with your small mind and spread it with your big mouth.

Calories are little creatures that live in your closet and sew your clothes tighter each night.

I don't have an attitude problem-You have a problem with my attitude and that's not MY problem.

I am not weird. I am a limited edition.

Be the kind of woman that when your feet hit the floor each morning, the devil says, Oh crap-she's up.

There's no time like the present to put it off 'til tomorrow.

From now on we are screwing things up my way.

I've lost my mind. I think my kids took it.

Being old doesn't seem so old now that I'm old.

I already want to take a nap tomorrow.

Never underestimate the power of stupid people in large groups.

There is no chlorine int he gene pool.

How important does a person have to be before they are considered assassinated instead of just murdered?

Brain cells come and brain cells go, but why do fat cells live forever?

If a deaf person has to go to court, is it still called a hearing?

Could someone ever get addicted to counseling? If so, how could you treat them?

If the Energizer Bunny attacks someone, is it charged with battery?

Why aren't apartments called togetherments?

Why doesn't Tarzan have a beard?

If you're one in a million, there are six thousand people exactly like you.

People used to explore the dimensions of reality by taking LSD to make the world look weird. Now the world is weird and they take Prozac to make it look normal.

I hope these made you smile a little.

However you do it, whatever makes you laugh, keep it near. Personally, I laugh much at myself. I honestly do some really silly things, like I'll be working on a project, remember I need something in the kitchen, head for the kitchen, get distracted, and not remember why I'm there. I stand there with a blank expression on my face, trying to recall what it was I was supposed to fetch. I find if I give up and laugh about it, I inevitably remember and finish my task.

I once got up, put on my pants inside out, and never noticed until I got to the office. Thankfully, there is a restroom immediately inside the door so I ducked in and fixed them. I'm not exactly senile yet, but I sometimes wonder at myself. The point is that humor is a weapon in your arsenal against fear. You can't laugh and be afraid at the same time. When you laugh, your body sends out endorphins that lift your mood. (We'll get into brain chemicals later.) When you start thinking of humor as a useful tool, you will see it's a necessity in your life.

And as I suggested before, go to my website, travelerpelton.com and head over to the "Something Funny This Way Goes" page-start reading next time you're down and I predict one of those are going to make you laugh! Drop me a line and let me know which one was your favorite!

Chapter 1-G
Run It Out

The seventh practical exercise is just that, exercise. Fifteen minutes walking outside can refocus you. Fifteen minutes of exercise inside can do the same. I go into this more fully in a later chapter, but I urge you to put exercise in your daily routine, even once you go back to work if you're one of those who are home right now. If you can't go out to walk, put on music, and dance at home; even if you think you have two left feet, you can make believe you're a ballroom dancer when there's no one around. Waltz around the room with yourself or if you have a companion, waltz together. (Wise hint, move the throw rugs. No need breaking something in the next step, step, slide routine.) Breath deep and move. If you have legs that work, get up and use them to refocus on just your body and how it feels to be released to move.

I have this thing on my wrist called a Fitbit-you don't need to get one of the same brand but I find I break this kind less. (I tend to do things like get it wet too often, or forget to charge them, I have dropped things on it and gotten kicked in the wrist my one of my alpaca-the devices tend to not like that. In the morning, it tells me I have gone 0 steps. My goal each day is to have that little band say at least 6000 steps, more if possible. On a really good day, I go over 10,000. It gives me a psychological lift to realize that it works, I work, and we are in this together. When I reach the daily goal, it lights up, vibrates, rings, plays little fireworks, and it makes me smile. It's one of those little things that isn't necessary but makes you feel a little sense of accomplishment.

If you are older or unable to walk, you can still do exercises in a chair; there are many leg lifts, arm lifts, stretches, that can be done while sitting.

And, by the way, music is an important tool as well. Music (and again, there is a chapter on why the use of music and other art forms help you relax) is a force for good in your mind. Many folks have an exercise playlist that starts out with a marching piece, goes into something a bit wilder and with more beat and ends with a slowdown piece; a playlist seems to help because you can make it fifteen or twenty minutes long, you know that when this or that song comes on you are almost done; it helps you relax and get into it.

If you can get outside to exercise, do it. The air inside a house can get stuffy; if it's possible, open the windows if you can't go outside. Simply walking around the block is good. If you are too weak to do that, just stand on the porch. Do five calming breaths; get the air into your lungs. Look at what's around, notice the neighbors across the street; see the neighborhood cats wandering around? Can you hear a dog barking, or an ambulance siren, or someone running a lawnmower? Now during your breaths, see what you smell- fresh grass from that lawn mowing, or flowers or just the smell before rain or after?

Do this before you leave your front porch or step; if it's all you can do, fine, go back in and call someone. If you can walk to the mailbox and post your letter and come back and that's all, fine. If you can walk to the corner and back, or run around the block, all good. Just get outside if you can a few times a week, preferably once a day. If you must be inside and have the equipment, use it. If you don't have any, did you know that a can of soup weighs a pound and you can use it to exercise your arms by lifting up and down slowly, like any other hand weight? There are many videos on YouTube with indoor exercise routines - the number of just tai chi online is astonishing. There are YouTube videos now for walking on your treadmill, so you watch the video and it seems like you are walking down a country road or at the beach while soothing music plays. I've used a few and they are lovely.

Exercise costs nothing but does so much for your body. Exercise makes your body kick in endorphins; endorphins make you feel good.

(One of my smaller clients called them dolphins once, told me she ran until she could feel the dolphins in her head swimming. I've always somehow remembered that child. She must be twenty or so now. And I agree, it helps to have dolphins in your mind.)

The important thing is to get moving, every single day, for at least twenty minutes. If you are ill or weak, then break it into two sessions, morning and evening. Build on it each day so as you grow stronger, you exercise for a few minutes longer.

I learned long ago that when I've had a stressful day, the best thing I could do was to grab my husband or my dog and take off for half an hour of wandering around my field. I'd start out walking way too fast, slow down and finally start noticing things, spring beauties just popping up in the field, the snapping turtle in the creek making his submarine forays, head above water, body submerged, a water wake following him as he cruised for prey, small minnows darting here and there, a new

47

nest of red-winged blackbirds next to that big honeysuckle bush at the corner of the backfield; halfway around the field, I'd slow down, I'd start breathing calmer, and realize that despite all the hurt in the world, it's still a pretty grand place to live. My husband Dan ambles along and when he sees me start to relax, he'll start a conversation on what's been going on at the farm while I've been at the office, and inevitably has something to show me-the kittens in the barn have their eyes open, the button quail have hatched, the rose of Sharon is budded out, ready to bloom. Life is good if you let it be.

Chapter 1-H
Reframe

The eighth suggestion is to reframe whatever it is that is making you feel bad today, this moment in your life. For example, if you are catastrophizing about your current situation when your mind sort of goes off on a tangent all by itself and you feel a little helpless to stop it, or you find yourself mentally taking things to the farthest, most horrible conclusion, something like, "Oh, boy! I have to stay home and stay in and teach my kids and balance the bills and we could catch a horrible disease and how will I pay for the funerals and what's going to happen to the government and can I learn to speak Chinese or Russian at my age? The world is ending!"

Whoa, there. You can reframe this line of thinking pretty simply. Turn each thought, each intrusion in your head, around. Reverse them, like this.

"Oh, boy! I get to stay home, sleep in a little, play with my children, take walks, and be my own boss for a few days. I don't have to put up with that crazy person who works next to me on the line or in the cubical; I will have unemployment and the bills will get paid but meantime, this is a vacation from the rest of the crazy in the world. I don't even have to leave the house. I sort of hope it goes on longer than I expect. It's spring and the weather is going to be great and I am going to be fine. In fact, I'm grabbing the kids and going for a walk. No need to stay in here and stare at the walls. And when we get back, I think I'll find our old monopoly game and start a three-day binge with the kids. Popcorn and homemade milkshakes for supper! Woo-hoo!"

Change how you read your circumstances and the stress level goes down. Learn from what's happening. Rather than stress because there isn't any toilet paper to be found to buy, remember you have toilet paper in the closet or where ever you keep it. If you honestly are completely out of the stuff, you can substitute something else a few times until you can get some. (Remember, for instance, when you were a baby, your mom used wet washrags to wash your bottom when you messed it? They are still available in most households, they can be washed in the washer and reused until you get some toilet paper. On your next foray out, if there isn't any toilet paper, then buy a bunch of cheap washrags, stack them neatly by the sink, dampen them before use and drop them into a bucket of bleach water until you have time to toss them in the washer. You can also substitute paper towels; just don't flush them. You can cut up a couple of old t-shirts and use them; they wash, they can be reused. That's what they did back before toilet paper was invented. You don't have to go pick leaves and use them. There are ways to get around the problem until things change.)

Being out of one modern convenience is not the end of all things. Instead of stressing about sanitizer, remember you have soap and water and it works fine. Take reasonable precautions, but don't let the hype fool you. You will survive this temporary inconvenience because that's all it really is, a temporary inconvenience. It's just not worth your peace of mind to worry about it.

Reframe whatever is the largest problem, cut it into small bits and you will conquer it. It will make you more self-sufficient, stronger, and capable.

You can then say things like, "See, figured that out. What's next?" You don't have to worry about what the neighbors think because they're in the same boat as you are and they aren't going to be in your bathroom anyway. They're stuck inside and making the best of it.

Reframe that thought; conquer that idea. Move forward.

Chapter 1-I
Kindness to You

We've seen eight practical ways to calm yourself, to ease your mind, to take care of yourself and this last thought is in order: be kind to yourself.

Don't allow inner voices programmed from childhood take over your waking hours. When a negative thought comes, take it to its logical conclusion and shut it down. When your head says be afraid, all these newscasters and forecasters must be right what's going to happen? Don't go there. Turn them off. Remember God is still in heaven; you are still alive and well on planet earth. It's not going anywhere and chances are, you aren't going to suddenly pass away.

This is not the time to obsess about other's opinions of you. It a time to build up, not down, to find a better sense of self; to say good things to yourself about yourself. Not, "Oh, I'm getting old and I'm at risk." No, it's "I'm older, but I'm wiser; I take care of myself, and I am not afraid of what today brings. I have lived through much to get where I am and I am going to live through this as well. I will be better on the other side, smarter, leaner, stronger. I am not what I was. He promised me personally,

"Be strong and courageous. Do not be afraid; do not be discouraged, for the LORD your God will be with you wherever you go." *Joshua 1:9*

You do realize you can combine all the above? You can use laughter and exercise, calming breathing and RAK all on the same day, together or after each other. We'll talk about some specific ways to make the days fill up with good things and eliminate the boredom of thinking there is nothing in your life to do and give you a structure that helps. But for now, those are the first eight practical ideas to start us on our journey.

Each one you can do. They are easily mastered, and need to become second nature for you. They cost nothing except time, and if you're home right now, you have time. Each one can make the day easier, lighter, and you stronger and more capable.

They are just the beginning salvos of our attack on the fear cycle. In order to totally control it though, you need to understand the storm that anxiety and fear causes in your body. Let's go into a little of what makes up fear and anxiety and all those other things that we'd like better control of in the next chapter. Lace up your boots, pick up your walking stick, pull on your hat, and get ready for some hard slogging! I promise it gets easier after this chapter! Deep breath, ready? Turn the page.

Chapter 2:
The Mechanics of Fear and Anxiety in Three Passes

Fear is an unpleasant emotion that happens when your mind feels you are in some sort of danger. It's also a normal emotion. Being afraid doesn't mean you're cowardly, or irrational: it means your body is operating within normal parameters; your brain reads danger, it reacts. It doesn't really matter if there is a real physical threat; your brain can react to something like missing a work deadline the same way it responds to something that's actually life-threatening, like a car crash or a tornado. You use the same parts of the brain, the same hormones, and endocrine glands to deal with any perceived threat. Whether taking your SAT/ACT or watching too many news reports about wars, riots, plagues, and earthquakes, your body has one set of chemicals to deal with them all. Your internal self has its own set of triggers to deal with the world around us and our perceptions of it.

Your brain is a wonderful mechanism. Your brain perceives four root emotions, mad, sad, glad, and fear. All other emotions are combinations of these four. At present, there seems to be much confusion over rational and irrational fear, over individual and mass fear. But fear is neither rational or irrational; it's just a state of being. So how does your body perceive fear? Let's get really basic first and then repeat the process each time adding a little to the network we're building in your head so you get a deeper understanding. It's a complex subject and I've found over years of teaching and working with people if you set a basic framework, you can then go back and add more information; the brain connects them and you remember it better; your comprehension goes up with rehearsal and additional facts.

First, the really basic version, just to give us a framework to hang other ideas from later.

Your brain sits in your head on top of the spinal cord that is attached to nerves coming from all over your body. Remember your health textbook when you were in school or your human anatomy book in high school or biology? Mine had these neat overlays inside the middle of the spine where each system of the human body could be layered on top of the one before and finally, looking through all the layers, you could see how marvelously the complexity is that makes us human.

When a baby is born, it doesn't have a lot of information on what could be dangerous, so it only is afraid of falling and loud noises. It has a startle reflex when it feels either of these and immediately cries. As you grow older, you learn other things that are uncomfortable, and your body makes use of each new thing you learn to build up a composite list in your head of all things dangerous. A dog bites, you learn to fear dogs; you touch a light bulb, it's hot, you fear bright shiny things. If your family is poor and you sometimes don't have food, you develop a fear of being hungry. Kids tease you at school, you learn to have less confidence, less self-assurance; someone laughs at you during a school performance or a dance recital or a game and you develop stage fright. You're in your first car accident and you shy away from cars that seem to be coming right at you, even if they're on the other side of the road. Your dad or some other adult yells at you or hurts you and you become afraid of angering men. All the experiences of life build up your mental triggers for fear.

Later, when something happens, a smell that reminds you of an abuser, or a sound that reminds you of an accident, or simply an unusual situation, your body reacts as it is programmed to do. And how does it react?

First, there is the trigger (scientists call it the stimuli); it puts your body on alert. In reaction, the amygdala (a small almond-shaped organ in your brain) sends out a cascade of orders to your body so you run away, set up to fight, or freeze. A whole series of things happen instinctively, and you don't even realize you're doing it.

Your pupils dilate so you can see better. Your perceptions heighten and come into sharper focus; you make judgments on escape routes or where to stand to fight. Your muscles tense up and you breathe more rapidly to build up oxygen to the muscles. Your adrenal glands (they're right above your kidneys) release a stress hormone called cortisol. It acts to improve perception, raises the heart rate and blood pressure, and tells your liver to release stored energy. When your muscles tighten, even your skin tightens – which is why we get goosebumps. If we were hairy animals, it would make us look bigger and fiercer because the hairs would stand up. Have you ever seen two cats fight? Their hair stands up, their eyes widen, they growl. Your skin tries to stand up hair but most of us just don't have enough body hair for that to work. We get goosebumps. Since we are all not hairy, we just look sort of like a chicken that's been plucked.

Your body shuts down non-essential actions (dare we say just like a government when fighting a pandemic?) Your digestion can slow way down or stop altogether. Your blood is forced into your major muscles and your brain. Adrenaline raises your body heat almost as if you have a fever.

One of the really interesting things that happen is that the frontal lobe partially shuts down. The frontal lobe is the part of your mind that processes rational thought. It takes a lot of energy to run rational thought, so the body sends that energy elsewhere. The part of your brain at the back is called the animal brain and it basically takes over. This is why sometimes when people are frightened, they appear to be angry as well; they are short-tempered and they can lose control – in some people, to the point, they actually blackout mentally and hurt someone or break something, and they don't realize it until afterward.

Fear is essential to our survival, but it seems to be a little trigger happy sometimes. If we have been raised in a constantly changing or chaotic home as a child, or if we were raised in a war zone or in a domestically violent family, our system works almost too well. It over-reacts with chemicals to the point that we actually damage our brains. Let's go back not with the framework we've made and go into the process a little deeper so we understand the how of it better, building on what we read before.

You have two brain systems, so to speak, the sympathetic and the parasympathetic. One sends you up, one brings you back down and reestablishes normal function. Go back to the beginning when I described the process quickly and let's fill it in. When something happens that triggers fear, your amygdala fires an order to the hypothalamus that then activates the pituitary gland, the pituitary gland secretes adrenocorticotropic (ACTH) hormone into the blood. The ACTH tells your adrenal glands to slurp epinephrine into the bloodstream. It also tells the body to drip cortisol into the system. The cortisol circulates throughout the body and turns fatty acids into energy so you can run or fight – it's like a jolt of hi-test to a car. More hormones, called the catecholamine hormones, including epinephrine and norepinephrine, prepare muscles for violent action. Non-essential services to the body are shut down; things like your digestive system, which you may read as feeling like you've got butterflies fluttering around down there. The production of tears slows down, you'll get a cottony, dry mouth, your hearing may be less but your eyesight focuses. Heart and lung activity goes up. You enter a stage called hypervigilance.

Your hippocampus, the brain part that is dedicated to memory storage, is in the inner region of the brain, right at the top of the brain stem, and controls emotional response. It kicks in to flip through your memories to figure out what to do and it actually helps control the fear response. Your prefrontal cortex, the part of the brain involved in high-level decision-making, works together with it to assess the actual threat.

If the hippocampus and prefrontal cortex decide that there isn't any real threat, or that you're actually enjoying this (think roller coasters and scary movie night with friends), the sensible "thinking brain" can overpower the primal parts of the brain's automated fear response. You calm down.

Our problem is that the brain doesn't differentiate between real and perceived threats – it overgeneralizes, allowing for the buildup of fear, which changes into anxiety. Anxiety is an emotional response to an imagined threat. It's really not bad to be anxious unless it goes on for too long or leads us to do irrational things.

Irrational things like when Washington State, which is where so many of the first Covid-19 cases started, began issuing alerts, some bright person realized that a good many of the toilet paper production plants were there. Some other bright person stated at one time that if Washington state shut down, so would our supply of toilet paper and the race to buy out the grocery store shelves was on. People bought huge stockpiles of the stuff assuming the worst. Washington State did not shut down. However, due to the panic buying, they couldn't make the stuff fast enough. There's plenty of it around. However, it's been hoarded. It's not on the shelves so when folks go into the grocery store, they see empty shelves and feel vindicated. It lasts until the next imaginary shortage occurs.

Now, Covid-19 does not normally cause diarrhea. It is a respiratory illness, but no one ran out and bought out the menthol salves until later when enough news programs talked about it being a respiratory illness. One by one, different things were suggested as possibly being in danger of running out, and people dutifully went out and bought out the hand sanitizer and the gloves and masks and then cough drops. Stores limited the number of containers of flu medication you could buy since someone suggested that you treat Covid-19 like the flu. I can't imagine how the stores are keeping things stocked since they don't know what the next panic run is going to be about. We develop hair-trigger responses to suggestions that may or may not be true. We have no way of actually knowing, so we panic and buy cases of bottled water and canned goods and frozen stuff; enough to last us for six months should everything shut down. It's all about the fear cycle in our brains short-circuiting our common sense.

Now let's go over it one more time and complete the filling in of the process.

Fear is a bodily chain reaction to a perceived threat. There are two parts to the autonomic nervous system – that is the automatic part, not controlled by conscious thought. It is the part of the nervous system controlled in the brain stem, the section in the back of your head, at the top of your spinal cord. The sympathetic nervous system controls the "go now" part of the system, gearing your body up for action, and the parasympathetic part of the nervous system tells you to slow down and allow everything to fall back into normal functioning. The parasympathetic nervous system controls the body at its normal "homeostatic" state of being in balance, working properly, and being at rest. The sympathetic controls the fight or flight responses. They balance each other out.

When there is a perceived danger, the amygdala sends messages to the hypothalamus through the sympathetic nervous system to start the flow of chemicals needed to get away from the threat or beat it into the ground with a club. The result is a very quick, very reactive set of physical responses to the chemical messengers being sent all over. After the danger is over, the parasympathetic system slows it all back down. You cannot stay in a state of hyper-awareness all the time. That has its own problems and can actually cause brain damage.

To get messages to many different parts of the body, the hypothalamus sends impulses through the sympathetic nervous system. The hypothalamus is sort of like a military drill sergeant, yelling out orders, (You, burn that fat! You, focus those eyes! You, more blood flow to the big muscles. Now, now, now). The sympathetic nervous system nerve impulses travel very rapidly through the branches of the sympathetic nervous system. The effect of the sympathetic nervous system on body systems is very rapid but quite brief. Epinephrine (also called adrenaline by some) dilates blood vessels, giving you goosebumps and more blood flow. It temporarily keeps you from feeling pain.

You've heard of police officers or soldiers who were injured themselves but didn't feel it until after they'd carried out other soldiers or civilian. When the danger was past, they suddenly realized they were bleeding. That adrenaline rush simply blocks the pain receptors from getting through because you have better things to at the time than worrying about an injury; you have to get out of there. Pain is considered by the sympathetic nervous system as something that can be put off, so it is.

In the meantime, cortisol slides into the blood system and increases blood sugar levels by converting stored glycogen and fats into blood sugar. Cortisol also suppresses the immune response and inflammation. You have a major hormone storm running through your blood system and it enables you to run away or fight the saber tooth tiger or, in some cases and with some people, you freeze. In nature, animals/birds/insects that have camouflage coloring will freeze in hopes nothing notices them. Deer fawns are set to bed by their mothers and they lie so still that unless you know what to look for, you see nothing. Some people do that as well. No, they aren't camouflaged but because of earlier experiences where they learned there was no use to run away, they were going to get hurt anyway, they react with total helplessness and just stand there.

Due to life experiences, they feel so overwhelmed, overpowered, or trapped, they freeze. I've worked with children who had been badly abused and had learned the futility of fighting the adults in their lives so they would send their conscious minds away and just stand or lie there and take the abuse. It's hard to bring them back to normal function, to teach that they can and should fight back sometimes.

Fear hormones result in a longer-lasting and more widespread fight-or-flight response than the effects of the nervous system. Your body cannot keep this up for long. You need it to shut down as quickly as possible. The parasympathetic nervous system restores homeostasis – that's what balance is called by scientists-and shuts down the sympathetic system. It makes you relax by telling all the differing glands to stop producing fear hormones.

Some people, because of the amount of trauma or chaos in their lives, have highly reactive systems that never completely shut down. It shrinks their hippocampus (a horseshoe-shaped organ that is responsible for long term memory and emotional response) and can cause memory damage.

Chronic stress increases the chance of health issues. If you were being chased by a lion and successfully ran away afterward, you'd be hungry and you'd eat. But in our modern lives, there are very few real saber-toothed tigers or cave lions, yet people stress-eat, causing weight gain and increasing their risk of health problems. For example, increasing a person's blood sugar due to anxiety can increase risk of diabetes.

Further, anxiety puts extra strain on the blood vessel walls leading to heart problems. When the fight-or-flight response causes blood pressure and heart rate to remain high, it puts extra strain on blood vessel walls. As a result, the linings of blood vessels can become damaged. An interruption of blood flow to the heart can lead to a heart attack. Blood vessels in the brain can also be blocked, resulting in brain-damaging strokes.

People suffering from stress secrete cortisol at much higher rates than normal people. There is evidence that abnormally high cortisol levels may be the initial trigger for depression in some individuals. High cortisol levels also result in sleep deprivation (lack of normal amounts of sleep). Stress also affects the function of the immune system, the body's natural means of fighting off infection. Stressed individuals produce lower levels of antibodies when exposed to pathogens. They also produce higher levels of cytokines, inflammation triggering chemicals secreted when fighting infections. Excessive inflammation is thought to increase the risks of heart disease, diabetes, and some forms of cancer. In other words, feelings may have serious health consequences.

Hearing the complexity and efficiency of just this one human body system brings to mind a verse that I learned in childhood:
"For You formed my inmost being; You knit me together in my mother's womb. I will praise You, for I am fearfully *and* wonderfully made; Marvelous are Your works,
And *that* my soul knows very well." *Psalms 139:13&14*

People were made a wonderfully complex and beautifully well-thought-out mechanism; everything works together, everything depends on each other piece. We were never meant to be alone, to live as hermits, and that is what makes our present situation with the pandemic so hard on some of us. Our bodies have a defense apparatus built-in, the wonderful sympathetic and parasympathetic nervous system. It's only when, due to circumstances, we overload that system that we get into trouble. It's when life runs and rushes at us, when there is continuous violence, when fear has become endemic to our culture, that our bodies start failing us from fear and we become trapped and our self-governing system starts to fail.

It's up to us to take that system back, to let it calm, to allow it to come to balance again through our actions.

It's a complex thing we do and understanding the why and how of it helps. Now we go on to more that can be done to slow the process of fight or flight or freeze down. We know the why of what is happening, so when we feel the process start in response to a trigger (or a stimulus), we know what to do. We need to become mindful of when we are overtaxing our bodies and get rid of whatever is doing the overtaxing, be it too many special reports on TV, or too much speculation by family and friends on social media, or the feeling one gets when entering a grocery store nowadays.

God never meant us to live in fear. In fact, back at Creation, He set up a plan to avoid all this heartache, to avoid panic and anxiety. Let's look at some more concrete things you can do to slow things down and in a later chapter, we'll explain what He originally set up.

That was a pretty hard hill to get up now, but you now have a good idea of what happens in your body and why. You may begin to see the dangers of constant fear and anxiety. Let's stretch a bit and walk back to the house for some tea before we continue the journey of understanding how to control that which has tried to control us. We've seen the mechanism of fear in our bodies, but what do we do about it?

Let's look at that in chapter three.

Chapter Three:
Coping with Fear

"The only thing we have to fear is fear itself." Franklin Roosevelt (and quoted by a lot of people.)

Perhaps the most important coping tool is to be kind to yourself. What advice would you give to a best friend about those negative inner voices that whisper: *Be afraid. Don't try anything new?* Do as you advise others; don't listen to the negativity; be your *own* best friend.

Fear is one of our most powerful emotions. We've seen that it has a very strong effect on your mind and body. It can fire up our defense system whether the threat is a physical one, like a tornado or pandemic, or a non-dangerous event like final exams, your first date, having to give the prayer the first time in church, or getting married. None of those things are apt to actually do you harm, but convince your cottony mouth and beating heart to slow down as your bride walks down the aisle towards you, or they hand out the ignominious little blue exam booklets. It is the body's natural response to any trigger that might be considered dangerous in any way.

Anxiety is the word used to describe fear that is totally mental or emotional. The thing that makes us worry may not even be possible of happening. We think there is a threat and our body goes on low alert and we wait for something to happen. You are on alert like a platoon of soldiers being told to keep their weapons ready and just sit there and wait to charge. Anxiety, the brother of fear, can sit on your head like a lurking beast, waiting to steal your confidence and keep you awake at night with its continuous nibbling at your mind. Short term anxiety, the kind you get the day before you have to give a speech and then passing when the speech is over, does you no harm and may actually increase your ability to do a good job.

Long term anxiety, in contrast, is the bad one; it's the one that can steal your sense of well-being. It prevents you from achieving what needs to be done, it keeps you from taking acceptable risks, like embracing the idea of getting a new job or proposing to the girl of your dreams for fear she'll say no, or keeps us from having children because we're worried we won't be good enough parents. Long term anxiety shortens your peace.

Some people become so paralyzed by fear or anxiety they allow it to overwhelm them. They need to break the cycle of fear and get back on their life journey, as you are doing by following the ideas in this book. I want to congratulate you on getting this far and encourage you to continue the walk down this path. The coping skills you need so you can live a better life are achievable. You are absolutely capable of doing them.

Looking at all the complexity of fear, how do you help yourself? In Chapter 1, we went over some beginning steps to help you start taking control. Let's continue the list of what you can do to settle your mind back to where it is supposed to be, not where you find yourself at present.

First, look at the thing you are afraid of directly and face that fear. Study whatever it might be and figure out why it is frightening to you.

Let's say you have a job review in the morning; have you done well at your job this year, given it your best? If you can answer yes, then put that fear aside, you haven't done anything wrong. Have you heard there are going to be lay-offs or cutbacks and you're expecting bad news? Whatever for? You do every year and they've never really hurt before – no one is going to feed you to the lions. And if there are lay-offs, firings, whatever, in the works and you honestly know there are, stop assuming it's you. Do what you can to lower your risk and be prepared. For instance, consider yourself forewarned if there have been problems in the business and start doing some proactive things to prepare like polishing up your resume, checking the status of your bank accounts and your bills, setting up a tighter budget.

Look at the real facts you have, that are provable, from reliable sources, not the gossip, scuttlebutt, or rumors. Using the job review example:

a) this happens once a year; it's not the first time I've been through this and it won't be the last

b) the other's ones were fine

c) I lived through them; I was not struck by lightning and I was not fired.

d) It takes more to train another person than it does to keep me

e) I am a competent, capable, and consistent individual; this company likes my work and there is nothing to worry about.

If, however, you have actually screwed up this year, can you do anything about it now? Of course not. You still need to polish your resume in case you aren't forgiven for being human and reaching the goals set for you, and make a plan for where you go next. Write a polite resignation letter, thanking them for having employed you (burn no bridges), letting them know you realize that you don't fit here well. If/when the boss says they are going to have to let you go, politely interrupt, tell him on reflection you realize you aren't a good fit here, so you have written a resignation letter for your file, you appreciate the chance to have worked for them but that you need to move on. Go out with class and style. Request a copy of your entire personnel file so you can learn from what has been written.

Thank him for his time and let him know that you will have your workspace cleared out by the end of the shift.

In other words, take care of the things you have control over, and put aside the things you can't and move on with your plan.

Let's look at something else you have no real control over; look at our recent pandemic. Look at it, but with rationality: what are the actual chances it's going to affect someone in your family or yourself? If you haven't been exposed, if you aren't working in healthcare, if you aren't in a high population area, then your chances of being affected are low. If you are one of the above, or a high-risk individual, then do what you can to remove as much risk as possible and leave it be. Let it blow over you. Be sensible, use precautions, but you have, I understand at this point when I am writing, a 1 in 51,000 chance of contracting it. And if you do get it, you have a 98% chance of survival. You cannot control the pandemic, nor the government's response, but do what you can do, be mindful of your own and your family's needs, and hunker down until it leaves.

There is a scripture verse that is making the rounds right now: I think it apropos for today.

Come, my people, enter your chambers, And shut your doors behind you; Hide yourself, as it were, for a little moment, Until the indignation is past. *Isaiah 26:20* (NKJV)

If you can compare this pandemic to a time of wrath, of anger against the human race for its destruction and mismanagement of this old earth, I think it makes sense.

Hide in your rooms, He tells us, until the fury, the plague, the wrath is over. Is God mad at us? No. However, He allows the natural consequences of our actions to happen: we made those choices, we pay for them. Something happened in China; right now the various stories don't agree on what and people get in over-heated debates over which one they believe. Shall we stay angry at China forever? There but for the grace of God go us; we could just as easily be the place where a similar thing started. God said to stay in where it's safe until the wrath, the indignation, the fury goes by. Shouldn't we follow His advice and the advice of the medical people? And if we are doing that, then what else can we do? Nothing. Therefore, do what is needed. Don't worry and fret, just keep soap and water handy; wear a mask, don't go out unless it's necessary. Do what you need to do. It won't last forever.

Remember that fear is a natural emotion. It is one way the mind has of coping with that which it doesn't understand completely.

Give your mind information and lower the apprehension. Don't internalize the fear by building on it. Don't read Facebook and expect to get good information; that's a little bit like going to the local sewing circle of old ladies or the gathering of old retired male checker players and expecting to get good clean gossip. It's fine for entertainment but take it with a large dose of skepticism. Look for information from trusted resources and make a rational decision on just how dangerous this is going to be for you.

Back when 9/11 occurred, there was much panic going on: how dangerous was it to be near cities, how we could get hit anytime. The government even put out a gauge of how dangerous something was going to be, this day might be listed as orange or yellow or green. All it did was exacerbate the fear. We know statistically that the chance of being killed in a terrorist attack is 1 in 2 million. In other words, yes, attacks happen, school shootings happen, but by and large, with the protections we have put in place – metal detectors, locked school doors, security guards – most schools are pretty safe. If it seems to be a danger in your area, then home-school your kids. Don't let something you can't control take over what you can deal with by just making a few changes.

If you avoid things that are uncertain and allow them to frighten you, you limit your happiness. Anxiety will increase if you allow yourself to make a pattern of avoiding things that *might* not be safe. Exposing the fear for what it is – often a lack of factual information – will stop those fears from taking you captive.

The second thing to ponder about the fear you have been feeling is to know yourself, your own abilities, your own limits. I worked with a middle-aged lady once who had never driven a car because she was fearful she'd have an accident. No one had taught her to drive, she was fearful of even trying, and it severely limited her life. If she couldn't walk to a job or get a bus there or someone to drive her, she couldn't take the job. Within walking distance of her home were fast-food restaurants, a nursing home, and a couple of small stores. No one was hiring. If she could drive just three miles, she had access to much better options. She came to me thinking she had a phobia about driving. I pointed out it's pretty difficult to have a full-fledged phobia when she'd never experienced driving. After teaching her how to physically relax, I convinced her to just sign up and take the classes at a driving school. She took the classes and took her driver's exam and wonder of wonders, got a permit.

For the next week, she was frozen, fearful of signing up for her driving practice. I asked her if she had a neighbor who drove and she did, and oddly enough they were good friends. I asked if she would mind bringing the neighbor to the next session, and she did.

We went out during the session to her neighbor's car. I asked my client to get in the driver's seat and just sit there. Then I asked the neighbor to explain what all the various parts of the cockpit were and what they were used for, which she obligingly did.

I then asked the neighbor if her friend could sit in her car once a day for the next three days, just feeling what it felt like. By the third day, the client felt a little silly not trying, now that she had gone so far, and made her appointment to take her first drive. Her neighbor allowed her to start the car, back it down the driveway and drive it back up the driveway and park it. The sky did not fall. She called the driving school who came out and picked her up that day; showed her how to adjust the mirrors, the seat, and back all the way out, watching for traffic. She drove around the block and stopped at all stop signs. She drove farther. At the end of the hour, they had her drive herself home. She was shocked. She called me when she got home and reported back that nothing happened. She drove for five miles, and the semi-trucks did not attack, the policemen didn't stop her. I told her to call the driving school and set up for the rest of her driving lessons. She made her appointments for twice a week for the next five weeks and finally took her test.

She passed. Her next move was to go to a vocational night school while working at a factory during the day. When I heard from her last, she was now working at a job she loved, she had her own car, was buying her own place, and was happier than she'd ever been. She faced her fear, she stared it down, and she succeeded in extinguishing it.

Fear is a bully; it backs you into corners and makes you quit. It lowers your expectations of just how good life could be. And, just like a bully, if you stand up to it, it eventually crumbles. Sometimes not without a fight, but it dies and you go on.

With some fears, sometimes it is helpful to keep a journal and look for patterns: when am I afraid? What was I doing when I started worrying? What did I think was the danger? By studying your own patterns of thought, you can adjust them. You can look at them and set small goals that you can do, breaking the big fear down into smaller, more easily defined steps.

I worked with a person who got panic attacks thinking of meeting new people. (I have her permission to share her story.) She was limiting herself to just those people she had known for years. The trouble was, people moved away, they passed away, they had their own lives to work on, and she was getting very lonely. She went to her job, came home, ate, fed her dog, watched TV, took a shower, and went to bed. Repeat. Repeat. Repeat. Saturdays she slept in late, then did her housework and laundry. Sundays she went grocery shopping. She worked in her yard. Once a month she visited her sister; once a week she visited her mom. She was bone-crushingly bored with her life. However, when we talked, it came out that as a child, her family had moved frequently and as the new kid, she had been bullied several times. It destroyed her confidence in the idea of making new friends.

We studied what happened to her when her panic attacks were triggered. I taught her to relax using the steps we went over in chapter one, breathing through it, relaxing her muscles deliberately. Then we discussed where might be safe places to visit to meet people. She listed a couple of places, one being church, another joining a local interests club (in her case, a quilting group), and volunteering at the public library or the cat shelter.

Her first assignment was to call each place and find out what time meetings occurred or what was expected of a volunteer and what sort of training she'd need. Since she decided to try church first, the next week, I had her go to the parking lot of the church and sit there for a few minutes, calming herself.

I had her choose the outfit she was going to wear. Since she was a crocheting person, I had her choose a very soft, silky yarn, a hook and simple pattern she already knew to take along, so that if she got nervous, she could quietly do something with her hands to distract herself. Other folks use a worry stone they carry in their pocket and rub, still others take along a roll of lifesavers and when they get nervous, take one out, put it in their mouth and concentrate on the flavor, not what is going on. The idea is to distract yourself from thinking of how you feel, from your fear about how you are being seen.

She was shocked to be invited to dinner by one of the church ladies. She asked if she might come next week and was told certainly. We set up in our next session to bring a small hostess gift, and a dish to share (a salad is safe, or a small dessert.) I helped her realize that she was a likable person, that this was a good thing. She went and found out that the other woman actually worked in another department of the same place that my client worked; they arranged to meet and eat lunch together. She was introduced to a couple of others and now has increased her network of friends. She can meet people without as much difficulty, and she has an outlet for when she feels lonely. She added good things to her life. She is now one of the greeters at her church; she invites people to her house. She volunteers at the cat shelter, helping to socialize the abandoned animals so they can be adopted out; she attends a quilt group once a month and loves seeing what everyone is doing. And she's recently started dating. She *really* never thought she'd do that.

In severe cases of panic and fear, there could, in some cases, be a chemical imbalance in your brain. For these types of anxiety, you need a visit to your own doctor to find out what medication will help you.

Remember the damage I mentioned before when someone has been under too much stress for too long? In these cases, it is sometimes necessary to go to a doctor and get a prescription to help you moderate the amount of hormones that your body is giving off. It's out of control and it takes time to get back under control; in addition, if you have a hereditary condition, like bipolar disorder or major depression, you may require medication to get your body's chemical balance to a healthy level. If, after you have honestly tried everything else, you find you are still in trouble with fear and anxiety, you might want to ask your physician to refer you to a therapist to work one on one for a while.

There is no shame in admitting that things are beyond your ability to fix. If you broke an arm or sprained your back, wouldn't you go to the doctor?

You wouldn't try to splint a smashed ankle by yourself. Sometimes, our minds need a professional to help us. Drugs are of most use when coupled with therapy. Drugs help balance your neurochemistry, therapy helps you examine your thoughts and reactions and puts you back in control of your own responses and life.

Your therapist may refer you to a local support group to try after a few sessions. Knowing that other people can have similar problems to what you are experiencing is a good and gratifying thing. You can see how others have been able to meet their challenges and they can be an encouragement. You can hear ideas and stories and what has worked for them and share what has worked for you; and you may even make some new friends. You will be doing them a random act of kindness by being there and listening with empathy, and they will, in turn, do the same for you.

Chapter 4
More Skills to Consider

Once you have become mindful of your fear, and have pinned down what trigger is causing the fear to wreak havoc with your well-being, you can look closer at what you can do to alleviate those fears. Setting your mind into a choice to not allow fear, anxiety, and confusion take control of your mental health and wellness is the first step. When you seriously learned the ideas in the first chapter was a second step.

Now let's look at some more advanced ideas. The first thing we need to look at is simply gratitude.

When fear starts rising in your mind and things look horrible for you, change the way you are thinking by starting to think instead of what you have to be grateful for; remember us speaking about thinking of your blessings? Instead of being afraid you have been asked to speak in public or teach a Church School class or substitute in a leadership role, instead of freezing or panicking, reframe what you are thinking into a gratitude sentence.

Instead of, "Wow! am I afraid of talking in front," think "What a privilege to speak to others about this experience. They are here to learn. I am going to do well, I've prepared, and this is an honor. That queasy bunch of butterflies down there better turn into hummingbirds because I am charged to do this! Deep breath, stand up, speak up, and shut up when I'm when done. Let's go!" You can do it: use self-talk to talk yourself out of fear.

When your mind is spinning in circles, try writing it down. Make lists.

Make a pro-con list: fold a paper in half, number along the edge of each side 1 2 3 4 5. Top of one side write "for" and the other "against". Then simply list the ideas without judging them on whichever side they belong. It can look something like:

Pro   Con

My job pays well	I hate the hours
The ladies' bathroom is nice	I hate being criticized all the time
The work isn't hard	That lady wearing that horrible perfume gives me a headache
I wish the boss wouldn't bring his dog to work	I really hate slobbery bulldogs
The guy who delivers the mail is cute	He's married

You can go on and on until it gets silly. But once you get it down, go back over it, take out the overtly silly ideas, the ones you can't do anything about, and then look at what's left. Studying it will give you an idea of which side you are really on and will help you organize the war in your mind from a rout into at least a less dangerous stand-off.

There comes a time when you need to just talk to someone, a friend, a relative, just another human being who will listen to you and who probably needs you to listen to them.

It seems like this one could have come sooner, but I am astonished at how reticent people are to talk to each other about something real to them, something that makes them feel vulnerable, as if that is something to be ashamed of. I know many times when I've had to stand myself up and ask myself, "Look here, it may not be just me feeling this way. It may be a lot of other people." Resist the urge to get on social media and throw it to the world. Find an actual human within reach that has an actual face you can talk to and better yet, a heart that listens. It can be a pastor, your mom, a friend, your husband, your girlfriend. It has to be someone who can hear you, who has a few minutes to listen as you talk to them. You need a flesh and blood, in the now, for-real human being for this step.

I sometimes tell people that I work with to take an index card and list all those people in their lives they could pick up the phone and call within the next 24 hours and ask them to hear them out on something. I tell them to keep it short but to get it down. I find, to my sorrow, that the overwhelming need in this world today is to be a listener. They are few on the ground. I am chagrinned at how often people come to me, a shrink, because they have no real human beings in their lives. Their folks have passed on, they have no relationship with sibs or relatives, their high school friends are long gone, and they have no church or club or organization to meet people. They have, in the daily rush of life, neglected their own lives. They come to me because they want the anonymity of a counselor with no relationship strings attached.

Friends, I have found from my clients, are messy things. If they listen to you, they expect you to listen to them.

The give and take of real friendship takes time away from work and video games and social media. But in living this way, we cut out the one thing that actually makes us human; relational communication. We have lost the art of just sitting comfortably in each other's presence with a glass of lemonade or a soda or cold water or tea – you would be surprised how you can hide behind something to drink – just sitting quietly and talking about what's of interest or of need to us. Just feeling for each other. You need people. I started this book telling you that people were never supposed to live as hermits and it is absolutely true.

This step may be the hardest for some of you. You might have to start with seeing a counselor if there is no one else you can trust or that you know. If it's a good counselor, they'll give you options and ideas of where to find friends and people, real people, around you. From churches to clubs, from service organizations to volunteering – they ought to know what's around in town where you can go to find a new friend or two.

If you are lucky enough to already have a living, loving parent, or a relative, or a good friend or two, then call them up and request a few minutes of their time and spill it. Tell them what's frightening you. In my experience, especially in a situation like we are in with the recent pandemic, they're probably having some anxiety as well, and you can encourage each other. Listen to your heart. Do what you need to do to find just the right person.

If you're getting more anxious day by day, being cooped up in your house hunkering down, and you've cleaned your nest, and you've journaled, and you still feel restless, then it's time to read. I don't think there is any place in the United

States right now without an online public library. The building might be closed, but you can go online and download five or ten books and read. You can email your local library and ask for suggestions on what's new.

There are still some open bookstores, not for browsing, but if you call or email them and request a certain book, you can order it and do a curbside pick-up if you have no books already in the house. I am constantly astounded at how many people don't have books in their house! I have a library, an entire room, with bookcases full and on long rainy afternoons, I don't get cranky or worried, I get lost.

I travel to India with Kipling, or Great Britain with Sherlock Holmes; I pull out quilt patterns and plan my next quilt; I read a cozy mystery or get totally lost in space with McCaffery or McKinley. If you have a good book, you can lose yourself in it for an hour or two or three and simply escape here for a while.

If you want to be motivated or to learn something new, there are millions of good non-fiction books – I have about 1100 myself on different topics – and reading the works of other minds on topics of interest is invigorating and stretches you in ways you would not think possible.

I remember one time we were snowed in and all the kids were home. Cable was down (we didn't have internet in those days!). Two kids were into crafts, so I hauled out a craft box, set them up on a table, and let them have at it. The older ones took off to read for a couple of hours. Occasionally, they'd come up for Oreos or apples and would give me some esoteric trivia they'd learned or want to read me a poem they'd found. I just kept making supper, cleaning around them, and let them go. Supper that night when Dad got home was amazing. They all had stuff to talk about. It was a long supper and a good one. Some of the odd facts I learned from or the other child:

Hashtags are actually called octothorpes.

In the fashion world, men actually wore high heels before women did and men originally did all the knitting and weaving.

Baby porcupines are called porcupettes; a group of baboons is called a congress, a group of flamingos is called a "flamboyance."

In 1916, Jeanette Rankin became the first female member of Congress in America, four years before women were given the right to vote.

Butterflies taste with their hind feet.

Tomato sauce was sold in the 1800's as medicine.

You get the idea. One child had memorized a poem she had to recite; two kids showed Daddy crafts they'd constructed for him. And at family worship that night all of them hoped the winter storm would hold on for another day because doing without was so much fun.

Talk to each other and read. You are missing so much if you don't.

Fear is created in your imagination to make your body take an action you might not really want to take. Instead of giving in to that fear and being miserable, do something. Do some other action, some other occupation. Get moving. Take a walk, read a book, call a friend, figure out a RAK to do for your neighbors. Maybe organize a front yard at six, everyone come out and check on each other from a distance – are we all ok? Take the dog to the park and walk. Or, for overachievers, try to walk your cat.

Take your kids to the country and look at the beauty of nature. Get out and ride a bike. Your fear fades as you move, as you accomplish something. So you live in a small apartment and it doesn't take much upkeep? Fine. The world outside could use someone with a garbage bag, a set of tongs, and the ability to walk around the block picking up the trash. Nothing is too outrageous to try as long as it's safe and legal. Sing out loud. Put on some music and dance. If you played an instrument in high school, polish it off, get it set up and play for a while. Don't let your imagination make you anxious. Give it something to do. Use your body to do it and sleep easier.

Instead of watching comedies or wildly improbable soap operas on TV, watch a documentary. Feed your mind. Don't let it wander off on its own, direct it, use it. Your mind is a marvelous thing, but it can get weaker without use.

Reading is good; but try making up a unit study on some topic and then watch a documentary on it along with reading a book on it. Someone once told me that if you read for a half hour a day, every day, on some topic, in a year you'd have the equivalent knowledge of someone with a bachelor's in that topic – you'd know it just as well as they without the expense of going to a college.

So, read that book, listen to that podcast, watch that documentary. Feed the brain. In many people I know, it's starving.

Chapter Five
Physical Skills

Sometimes we shoot ourselves in the foot by not looking at some of the easiest things that we can do to improve our chances of living a fulfilling, happy life. We make the huge assumption that our bodies have nothing to do with our minds or our emotions, and that could not be farther from the truth. Your body affects your mind on so many levels, and if you take care of one, the other works much better.

Many years ago, I learned this little mnemonic device to remember the eight most important things needed to stay physically healthy. (Of course, my grandson has a bumper sticker that says Exercise, eat right, die anyway, but he has got the oddest sense of humor...)

Research has s shown that people who follow these simple eight ideas live longer, are healthier, and have less depression and anxiety than the general populace. If these steps were expensive, or hard, or mentally taxing, I would understand better why people don't do them. I am convinced after working with people for over 25 years that what keeps us from doing them is simply a) laziness or b) we don't believe they will work or c) we don't know about them.

The eight rules look like this:

Sunshine

Temperance

Exercise

Water

Air

Rest

Diet

They spell STEWARD, so it's easy to remember them.

Let's take them one at a time.

Sunshine: Getting enough sunshine increases the amount of vitamin D your body creates. Vitamin D helps protect you from heart disease, prostate cancer, and dementia. Sunlight triggers the release of the hormone serotonin in your brain which makes you more alert and relaxed. Darkness triggers the release of melatonin which makes you sleep.

We sometimes treat people with depression by having them sit for a certain amount of time every day in front of a bank of bright lights. Bright, full-spectrum light causes a reaction in your retina which triggers the hormone, so the bright lights used in phototherapy trigger serotonin. The way our body reacts to light is called circadian rhythm. When you don't get enough light, your mental cognition is less pronounced, your memory is not as good; in general, you aren't as healthy.

I advise some of my clients who are prone to Seasonal Affective Disorder (SAD) to get full spectrum daylight light bulbs for all the lamps in their house; then to set all their lights on timers so they have at least 12 hours of bright light in the period of cold weather when they may not be able to get out.

Sunlight lifts your spirits. Vitamin D helps protect you from depression, it lowers blood pressure. Yes, I know the direct sun has gotten a bad rap in recent years, I am not suggesting you stay out in the sun for hours, but if you can get outside in the sunshine for twenty minutes a day, preferably in the morning while doing some exercise, it can do you a world of good.

Temperance: This is an old-fashioned word that simply means to be moderate in all things, very careful in the use of drugs and alcohol; use them in very strict moderation if at all. I know the scriptures say take little wine for your stomach's sake. I know the story of Jesus making huge water jars full of wine for the wedding in Cana. I know Noah planted a vineyard and got thoroughly bombed after the flood. I remain unconvinced of the goodness of alcohol.

I work every week with people who haven't been careful, who have the OC gene and are more apt to addiction, who have allowed drugs and alcohol to take over their lives, their homes and lost it all. Had they not tried that first hit, that first beer, that first cigarette – I can't tell you how many times people have broken down in my office with the "if only" diatribe. I have seen what it does to families. I have seen what it does to careers and self-esteem and health. I had a cousin, a good man who smoked for years. He spent the last years of life dragging an oxygen tank around his home so he could breathe; he had emphysema. Until you have spoken to someone with that disease or lung cancer or throat cancer or one of the other cancers cigarettes cause, you can't see how terrible life can become. I think we need to be extremely circumspect about what we drink or use.

An occasional glass of wine with a meal, or at a wedding, yes, I suspect there is a place for that. Heroin, cocaine, meth, cigarettes; I don't see a use.

I am told the reason people use drugs or alcohol to excess is to escape a grim life; how do you escape something by making it worse? My advice, stay away. Respect your own body, your family, your budget, and your life by taking better care of it. One of my cigarette smoking friends told me she smokes two packs a day; she's been doing it for a while, and you develop a tolerance and need to have more, as with any drug. Two packs a day times 365 days a year times the average of $7 a package means she is spending over five thousand dollars a year, literally going up in smoke. If you saved that up, you could take a seven-day cruise for thirty-five hundred and have lots left over to buy a wardrobe to wear and lots of souvenirs. What kind of computer/entertainment system could you buy for that sort of funds?

Moderation in all things; you may be a complete teetotaler and have a problem with online shopping, or too much exercise, or collecting salt and pepper shakers or eating chocolate or drinking soda. Whatever is throwing your mind and body out of balance can be an addiction. Look at your habits; figure out if they are reasonable in the light of society. Make adjustments to live more peaceably.

Exercise always seems to make most folks groan. Most of the people I work with don't like exercise very much, which helps explain why they have some problems with anxiety and depression. Exercise makes your body kick in endorphins, the feel-good hormone that lifts your spirits and gives you extra energy.

How much exercise? I tell my clients, who are sometimes not used to this at all, to start small: walk five minutes one way, turn around, walk back. Every two days add a minute to the walk until you can walk fifteen minutes one way and back, yes, thirty minutes a day, every day.

Walking doesn't take a bunch of equipment. It doesn't cost anything; I would assume you own shoes and there's a sidewalk or a park somewhere that's available. The benefits are enormous. One study reported that walking this way burns calories, strengthens your heart and lungs, helps lower your blood sugar, eases joint pain, boosts your immune system, and your energy, improves your mood, and extends your life. Walking thirty minutes a day will burn 1000-2500 calories in a week (depending on how fast you walk and the size of your body), which can help you lose weight. And did I mention it's free? What have you got to lose?

Water is overlooked so often because it's just here. We are blessed in the United States, most of it, to have safe water easily available. Your body is 60% water. Water improves your brain function, maximizes your physical performance, cleans your body (inside and out), relieves constipation, reduces the number of headaches you suffer, can help prevent or pass kidney stones, eases hangovers (hangovers are caused by the dehydration effects of alcohol, and rehydrating helps. I do not mean for you to go out and get drunk so you can drink water, but just a helpful hint here.) It can help you lose weight because it increases your metabolic rate – the National Institute of Health said that for 90 minutes after drinking a large glass of water, your metabolism is still up by 30%. Higher metabolism equates with higher fat burn.

And of course, you could also bike, swim, go to a gym, dance-just whatever it is, move.

Air is also overlooked. I mean, as long as you're breathing, you are fine right? However, as I pointed out in the first chapter, breathing in deeply and blowing out fully clears your mind, resets your mental compass, increases the oxygen to your brain. Breathing clean, fresh air and deliberately breathing deeply several times a day – not just maintenance, shallow breathing – improves your lung capacity. The air closed up in a building gets stale and can develop a less-than-ideal oxygen to carbon dioxide balance after a while; try opening a window or going outside.

Rest for some reason is looked down on nowadays. People seem proud that they only sleep four hours a night or make do with five hours. They are so wrong. Sleep is highly necessary for everyone.

Sleep clears your mind, improves your reflexes, focuses your attention. Insufficient sleep impairs higher brain function, like problem-solving and attention to detail. It makes you less productive and more likely to have a car accident. It influences your mood negatively, which can cause you to interact less kindly with other people.

Sleep deficits have been shown to be a factor in developing depression. Sleep affects growth and hormones, the immune system, your heart; lack of sleep increases the chance of obesity, infections, and general health.

During sleep, you go through cycles. Each cycle includes periods of very deep sleep and REM (random eye movement) sleep, which is when we dream. This pattern of stages is vital to our mental health.

I explain it to my younger clients this way: all day long when you are up and going to school or playing or whatever, your mind is taking lots of pictures and recording them; it tosses all those things on the floor of your mind. When you go to sleep, it's as if a little man were coming out to sort them. He works sorting out everything into the file cabinets, that is, your memory. Occasionally, he comes across something that there isn't a file drawer for, so he tosses it back up to the next level and tells them to figure it out. That's why you may have a dream about things that happened that day but skewed a little.

For instance, say you had to give a speech at school, and it scared you. That night, you might have an odd dream about standing in front of a bunch of people while naked, because that's how you felt up there that day. Or if you were frightened by a dog, you might have a dream about a huge monster dog. It's the way the body sorts the memories and then tosses them back to the file clerk of your memory and tells him where you want it stored. If your brain doesn't have enough time to work, the pile on the floor doesn't get sorted and you lose memories.

Sleep deprivation studies have found after so many hours of no sleep, people lose their ability to reason, they can hallucinate, some even develop psychosis.

On average, adults need 8 hours of sleep a night, teenagers 10 hours, babies 16 hours, children about 10 hours. Even allowing for individual differences, the correct amount of sleep ought to be one of the goals we set for ourselves.

Diet has a huge impact on how you feel. Processed foods, sugars, and chemicals in foods have surprising effects on our emotional well-being. Eating foods as close to what they originally were, be it a fruit, vegetable, nut, or grain, ensures we get as much of the good nutrition we need and less of the bad. I tell people they need to eat the rainbow; by that, I mean stick with colorful fruits and vegetables, lots of green things. They need the browns of nuts and golds of grains. To make it simpler for my clients I tell them to eat a salad a day with very little dressing. They need some protein at breakfast, lunch and dinner and a couple of servings of vegetables and fruits. Keep sweets few and small. I encourage them to stay away from white things – potatoes and white rice and white breads and pastas, and go for something not so washed out. If you eat food that is not so processed, you ought to get plenty of fiber. If you can get yourself used to eating many fruits and vegetables raw, good for you!

I personally don't eat meat; if it had a mother or a face I don't eat it. That's not for everyone, I know. I get most of my protein from dairy, nuts, and seeds. I would love to say I am tall, thin, and lithe but I'm not. I'm a grandma and I look like one. Yes, I bake cookies for the grandkids, and yes, we have pasta occasionally. Most of the time, we balance our foods out and eat simply and it has done us both (me and my husband) good.

I was raised to consider these with items as the building blocks of a healthy body. If I would add one more, it would be having faith in a Higher Power. I find that people who don't think of themselves as the be-all and end-all of everything, who look up to a Spiritual Power, seem better balanced and more resilient.

I suppose we could add a letter S to our word Steward, "S" standing for Spirit.

People with faith in something bigger than themselves tend to have an easier time learning to take things more in stride and flip over bad things that happen and look at it from another side.

For instance, "we have to stay home," flips over to "Great!
I can get the sewing room cleaned out finally!" Not," oh, no, what will I do? I have to stay at home." "I've been laid off? What is going to happen to me?" can be turned over into, "I've signed up for unemployment, we'll tighten our belts and God will help us get through this together". The attitude we choose to take towards an event helps us get through the event.

Having a faith in God gives your life perspective. As humans, we tend to be pessimistic; we have a major tendency to look on the bad side of things. I saw a guy with tee shirt the other day that proclaimed, "It's not half full or half empty. I drank it. Deal with it." A little in your face maybe, but with a good point. Don't focus on the fear or the trigger. Focus on what the next step is going to be; where you go from here and what's going to make it better. Having faith in God helps you do that by looking at a broader perspective. If this life is all there is, then how can we bear how fast it goes by? If we have eternity, then this life is just a place to learn to live morally and kindly and forever look for the lesson in what is happening. Either perspective is healthy. One is more comforting. Our perspective allows us to have more control over the life we have.

Are we able to stop all bad things? Of course not, I could get hit by a truck tomorrow; I can't control trucks or truck drivers. I could come out of remission: I don't have control over cancer; however, I beat it back once, and I'd do my darndest to do it again. Have I not failed at things before? Of course, I have, you have too! It is not the end of life as we know it.

You don't give up. You go on; you learn the lesson and you move on.

Having faith in God means surrendering the need to be in total control of the universe by yourself. It's a way of saying, I know I can't do everything. I am not giving up, but I am giving it to Him to handle and I will simply wait for Him to show me the next step. I do all I can, then I hand it over. When I am surrendered, I find peace. I am not the one who needs to make these decisions. I make decisions over what I actually have control over, and I have a better idea of what those areas I can control are. The rest is for someone else to do.

Can I control the Covid-19 virus? I hardly think so. What can I control in this situation? Where I go, who I am with, washing my hands, taking precautions, making my nest comfortable and clean. I can control what I buy. I can control right here where I am. Do I run the US government? No. Do I run the HHS department at the Federal level? Heavens no. Can I control what the state health department does or make decisions for them? No. Give that back to them. Take care of what you can and let it roll off your shoulders.

Now having said that there are instances when you do need to get involved.

You need to vote, that's in your power.

You may need to write letters about something to a government agency. You always stand up for principle. You always dare to defend your truly believed convictions. You have the right to peaceful protest.

The rest, let's say it's good to be informed, it's bad to let that information drive you to despair. It's simply data to sort and put away in the mental files until you can do something with it. Surrender the need to have total control over the world. You will never get it, so control what you can control. Give up your illusion that you can conquer the world and you free up your mind to focus on what is available to do. Pray for guidance. Perhaps God will lead you to someone who had the same problem you had and overcame it. They can give you pointers on what to do.

Sometimes, it helps to look at something and take it to extremes in your thoughts. Ask yourself What is the worst that can happen here? Is this going to actually kill me? Is it going to impact the planet? Is it going to ruin my life forever? Chances are the answer will be no.

Sometimes, by mentally taking it to its furthest extreme, you can laugh at it. One of my teenagers comes in from hanging out with buddies and he looks like a whipped puppy, drooping shoulders, head down, walking slow. He slumped into the living room, fell into a chair, and just sat there staring into space.
"Mom, I am never going to get married," he announced.
"Really?"
"I just lost the only chance I'll ever have." This from a fifteen-year-old.
"Really?"

"She dumped me for another man. And he wasn't even as good looking as me. He can't do math. He wouldn't comprehend ladder logic if it bit him in the butt. He hasn't got a part-time job or a bank account or anything. I just don't get it. I thought she was the one."

After all this teenage emoting, which I allowed to go on until I got tired of it, I pointed out that first of all, he hadn't graduated from high school, second, he didn't have control over anyone else and she obviously saw something in the other guy he didn't have, and finally, he hadn't done his chores, get outside and mow the back yard.

I guess that sounds heartless, right? But I had to get him out of himself and the act of exercising, taking out the frustration on something, then coming in, taking a shower, eating a good supper, interacting with sibs, took his mind off it. He got over it. Did he miss his chance to ever marry? Shall I show you the pictures of some of the cutest grandkids in the universe? I have a phone full of them.

What is horrible today will pass. My son had to understand that sometimes we get what we want, sometimes we fail.

Understanding we can fail, it's human, it's going to happen to us all, frees us up to try something else. I read somewhere that Edison tried 3000 times or more before he got the electric lightbulb right. When asked about it, he said he simply knew 3000 ways now that it wouldn't work.

Failure is only failure if you allow it to be.

Chapter 6
Other Considerations

In our quest for things to do or changes to make to enable us to be more at peace and gain a sense of serenity in the society we live in today, and mindful that none of us are just cogs in the great wheels of commerce, let's take a short look at some of the really interesting research that is being done about the creative side of our minds. Yes, when people think research, they think hard reading, boring statistics, and mind-numbing boredom. I suspect you all learned this from school as kids; the experiments in lab classes were always more interesting than reading the book to most kids.

Let's start by looking at the parts of our lives that schools always seemed to cut first when there were budget cuts, the things we take for granted. Music has major effects on our emotions, our health, our physical performance. Let's learn about the benefits music gives to you first, then the other arts.

In starting my research, I found hundreds of articles to read. Here are the most salient points about the specific benefits music may provide for your mind, according to the work being done by many different researchers.

Music can:

· Reduce depression symptoms. If you feel blue, music may help boost your mood. (retrieved from https://www.ncbi.nlm.nih.gov/pubmed/20013543) The kind of music matters; meditative and classical formats help many people feel uplifted, while genres like heavy metal may make you feel more depressed.

· Boost cognition. Research has found that background music may improve performance for test-takers, implying that it may influence other cognitive tasks as well. Individuals listening to music were able to finish more test questions during the allowed time, and they answered more questions correctly. (retrieved from
https://www.ncbi.nlm.nih.gov/pubmed/9450304)

· Lowers stress levels. A medical abstract showed listening to music may trigger stress-reducing biochemicals in your body. Music may also reduce stress specifically related to surgery. (retrieved
from https://www.ncbi.nlm.nih.gov/pubmed/21767754)

· Betters your mood. Research has found that music may help you get in touch with your feelings, and you may find yourself in a better mood as a result. (retrieved from
https://www.ncbi.nlm.nih.gov/pmc/articles/PMC3741536/)

· Improves your performance under pressure. One study found that upbeat music helped basketball players who had a tendency to perform poorly when they were under pressure. (Retrieved
from https://www.ncbi.nlm.nih.gov/pmc/articles/PMC3741536/
)

I did another search and found well over 2000 articles on the influence of music on your mental and physical health. The question you have to wonder is <u>why</u>? How does something simple to listen to and generally in the background have such an effect on our bodies? I am so glad you asked. Here I am putting on my professor hat now (I imagine it to look somewhat like a deerstalker) as we delve into this topic just a little more.

First, let's look at the actual physical thing we call music. Almost every culture in the world has some sort of music from towering Bach fugues to simple aboriginal flutes to drums to hip-hop and jazz. Music itself, in a physical sense, is simply vibrations that come to our eardrum and make it rattle. As the sound waves hit the eardrum, they are relayed along a chain of tiny bones in your ear, the hammer(malleus), anvil(incus) and stirrup(stapes). The stapes transmits the vibration to the cochlea which is sort of like a coiled-up snail shell. Inside the cochlea are ten to fifteen thousand minuscule hairs called cilia. The sound waves make the hairs wave back and forth which releases chemical neurotransmitters that activate the auditory nerve, sending electric currents to the temporal lobe of the brain. (The temporal lobe is located on both sides of your brain about halfway down). From there, stuff gets complicated.

Scientists, using PET scans and MRI scans, tell us that different parts of the brain sort different parts of sound. In other words, music has to be decoded for us to enjoy it. They tell us a small part of the right temporal lobe is responsible to perceive pitch, chords, and harmony; (Pitch makes melody, different patterns of pitch over time is melody; harmony is the combination of melody).

Still another part of the brain is responsible for sorting out timbre – that is, the quality that allows us to figure out what instrument is being played, i.e., what lets us recognize that flutes sound different than strings. Still another part, the cerebellum, processes rhythm. The frontal lobe sorts out the emotion in the music, while music that thrills your heart and sends your mind flying, (Think Vangelis' Chariots of Fire, or the prayer from Les Misérables) lights up the brain's reward centers.

Any healthy person does all this without consciously trying, but science has shown that musicians seem to be wired especially to perform all the complex tasks and understand and use the vibrations that make music into something wonderful. On the other hand, people who are mildly brain-damaged might not be able to perceive pitch at all (we call them tone-deaf.)

A couple of years back, there were many articles written about the "Mozart effect." Do you remember all the hype about playing Mozart to your belly while pregnant, and later once the baby is born, playing it for your child in an attempt to raise his/her IQ? Scientists were bemused by the fact that many musicians seem to have an easier time with mathematics so the University of California at Irvine designed a study to find out why. They gave a group of average college students a short IQ test, then had one group listen to a Mozart piano piece and another group list to soft environment relaxation tapes. They then took another short IQ test. Mozart won hands down no matter how many times or how many students from whatever place, Mozart won. They then tested to find out if it was just Mozart or did other music, say jazz or rock, have the same effect. Mozart won again. The kids listening to Mozart had increased special reasoning capacity after just ten minutes.

Now lest you get all excited, let me explain it is a temporary gain: it lasts about fifteen minutes and only lifts the IQ 8 to 10 points. Still, nothing else seemed to have that effect. It was enough that a whole bunch of entrepreneurs sold a whole lot of Mozart for babies CD's and made a ton of money. It still intrigues psychologists and there is more study going on. What can be concluded is that music improves cognition. It improves performance of your brain and gives a boost when you need it.

Can music reduce stress in these difficult circumstances like the ones we are going through as a country right now or the ones you are going through, whatever they might be? Several trials going on right now show promising results.

A study from New York of forty cataract patients with an average age of 74 who volunteered for the study. Half of them were given routine care. The other half chose music they liked ahead of time and they listened to it under headphones during their procedure and after their operations. Both groups had similar blood pressure two weeks before the proceedings, around 129/82.

Right before their procedure, it rose to an average of 159/92. That's pretty much expected, no one likes surgery! Then things changed. During the procedure, those receiving routine care without music retained the higher blood pressure the entire time. The blood pressure of the people with music playing through headphones dropped back to nearly normal in the recovery room.

Another study of 80 patients undergoing urologic surgery under spinal anesthesia found that music can decrease the need for supplementary intravenous sedation. In this trial, patients were able to control the amount of sedative they received during their operation. Patients who were randomly assigned to listen to music needed less calming medication than those assigned to listen to white noise or to the chatter and clatter of the operating room itself.

In the cataract and urologic surgery studies, the patients were awake during their operations. But a study of 10 critically ill postoperative patients reported that music can reduce the stress response even when patients are not conscious! All the patients were receiving the powerful intravenous sedative propofol, so they could be maintained on breathing machines in the intensive care unit (ICU). Half the patients were randomly assigned to wear headphones that played slow movements from Mozart piano sonatas, while the other half wore headphones that did not play music. Nurses who didn't know which patients were hearing music reported that those who heard music required significantly less propofol to maintain deep sedation than those patients wearing silent headphones. The music recipients also had lower blood pressures and heart rates as well as lower blood levels of the stress hormone adrenaline and the inflammation-promoting cytokine interleukin-6.
(Retrieved from
https://academic.oup.com/brain/article/131/3/866/318687)

You don't have to be a neurophysiologist to understand that music can affect the brain and at least a few of its many functions. And even if you're not a cardiologist, you may be interested to learn that music can also help the heart and circulation.

Doctors tell us that music can enhance the function of neural networks, slow the heart rate, lower blood pressure, reduce levels of stress hormones and inflammatory cytokines, and provide some relief to patients undergoing surgery, as well as heart attack and stroke victims. But these biological explanations and clinical observations may not do full justice to the effect music has on man and his world. Fortunately, poets and philosophers can fill in the gaps.

Doctors tell us that social isolation is a cardiac risk factor, and Robert Browning wrote that "He who hears music feels his solitude peopled all at once." Psychologists tell us that expressing emotions is healthful, and Tolstoy explained that "Music is the shorthand of emotion." Clinicians teach that human warmth can blunt many woes, and Shakespeare proclaimed, "If music be the food of love, play on." And in the days when belief in Apollo (who carried a lyre everywhere) reigned, Plato explained that "Music is a moral law. It gives soul to the universe, wings to the imagination, and charm and gaiety to life and to everything else."

Still unsure of the power of music? Listen to quotes from these other studies I found in my search:

"272 premature babies were exposed to different kinds of music – either lullabies sung by parents or instruments played by a music therapist – three times a week while recovering in a neonatal ICU. Though all the musical forms improved the babies' functioning, parental singing had the greatest impact and also reduced the stress of the parents who sang."
(retrieved from https://journals.sagepub.com/doi/abs/10.1177/0305735613499781)

105

You never knew there was a reason behind all those lullabies that nearly every culture has in some form? Music does babies good! And there is nothing quite so comforting as cuddling a little one and singing Puff the Magic Dragon or Jesus loves me as the baby goes to sleep. It's good for both of you.

"In another study involving surgery patients, the stress-reducing effects of music were more powerful than the effect of an orally-administered anxiolytic drug."
(Retrieved from
https://www.ncbi.nlm.nih.gov/pubmed/19388893)

Another study from Massachusetts General Hospital found that listening to Mozart's piano sonatas helped relax critically ill patients by lowering stress hormone levels, but the music also decreased blood levels of interleukin-6 – a protein that has been implicated in higher mortality rates, diabetes, and heart problems.
(Retrieved from
https://greatergood.berkeley.edu/article/item/five_ways_music_can_make_you_healthier)

". . . caregivers and patients with dementia were randomly given 10 weeks of singing coaching, 10 weeks of music listening coaching, or neither. Afterward, testing showed that singing and music listening improved mood, orientation, and memory and, to a lesser extent, attention and executive functioning, as well as providing other benefits.
(Gerontologist. 2014 Aug;54(4):634-50. doi: 10.1093/geront/gnt100. Epub 2013 Sep 5. *Cognitive, emotional, and social benefits of regular musical activities in early dementia: randomized controlled study.)*

Music does your heart good, your soul better. So my assignment for you is to find music you enjoy that uplifts you and listen while you're working, playing, resting; just surround yourself with one of the best gifts we have, music.

Whether we totally understand why or how it works is immaterial. What is important is that it is one more tool in our arsenal against anxiety and depression, one more step towards being the best we can be in this life.

What about other forms of art, things we may have taken for granted?

Drawing, painting, or molding objects from clay has been scientifically proven to help people to deal with different kinds of trauma. In a comprehensive article on *The Connection Between Art, Healing, and Public Health,* Heather L. Stuckey and Jeremy Nobel say that "[a]rt helps people express experiences that are too difficult to put into words, such as a diagnosis of cancer." "[A]rtistic self-expression," they continue, "might contribute to maintenance or reconstruction of a positive identity." (Retrieved from https://www.ncbi.nlm.nih.gov/pmc/articles/PMC2804629/)

In my work with people who have had a crisis or a severe trauma, like a car accident, a death, a divorce, domestic violence – the gamut of things humans manage to do to ourselves and each other in this world, if I can get that person to pick up a journal and start writing about that experience and then write again and then once more, they can heal.

The act of getting it out when there are no words they can use to tell another person verbally, the act of drawing a picture or pounding clay or writing about it, the rehearsal of the event gets easier and the person heals faster. This going over the event in a way that gets it out of their nightmares allows people to come to terms with it, to integrate it into their own story, their autobiography of themselves. It helps them make a meaning for it in their lives and they can look back at it, since it is over, and say, "it was hard, but I survived. I am whole again. I go forward. That event was terrible, but I learned from it and now I win."

One qualitative study that interviewed male survivors of childhood abuse found that asking them to write about their traumatic experiences allowed them – in conjunction with specialized trauma therapy – to make sense of the trauma in deeply personal ways. (Grossman, F. K., Sorsoli, L., & Kia-Keating, M. (2006). A gale-force wind: Meaning making by male survivors of childhood sexual abuse. *American Journal of Orthopsychiatry, 76*(4), 434–443. https://doi.org/10.1037/0002-9432.76.4.434)

Creative expression, art - be it writing a diary or a journal of rough times, or painting, sculpting, knitting, woodcarving, sewing, whatever you do to create – enriches our lives, relieves our stress, and enables us to be a stronger person.

Another thing that creating is able to do is help you with doing your daily RAK. Let's say you enjoy doing woodburning. You can think of your next-door neighbor or someone you know, make them a woodburned picture and gift them with it. You both receive pleasure. My daughter knits prayer shawls that she gifts folks with. I hand-spin yarn from my alpaca and gift my fellow crochet friends with something really fun to work with. I know a woman who has dozens of stamps; she stamps cards, colors them in with colored pencil and sends them out to people, one a day. She enjoys the art, her recipients enjoy the note, it's a win-win for all. Don't pass art by; don't pass up this easy thing you can do for yourself and others.

Coloring is not just for kids anymore. Have you seen the lovely adult coloring books available in scads? And this sounds wonky but I recently discovered I enjoy putting together jigsaw puzzles, gluing them together, framing them and gifting them to people. So far, no one has been displeased with them. It's an interesting conversation opener!

And a final idea to try:

Gardening

This is one of my personal favorites. As those of you who follow my Facebook page, Springhaven Croft know, I love gardening. In winter, I bring in all the houseplants and flowers like geraniums and impatiens and keep the flowers blooming all winter inside. In summer, the gardener in me strikes out and I am forever trying something new and different. I am pleased to say that it isn't just the country in me; it's therapeutic as well.

"Studies reported a wide range of health outcomes, such as reductions in depression, anxiety, and body mass index, as well as increases in life satisfaction, quality of life, and sense of community" (Retrieved from https://www.sciencedirect.com/science/article/pii/S2211335516 301401)

"Why does gardening seem to be so beneficial to health? It combines physical activity with social interaction and exposure to nature and sunlight. Sunlight lowers blood pressure as well as increasing vitamin D levels in the summer, and the fruit and vegetables that are produced have a positive impact on the diet. Working in the garden restores dexterity and strength, and the aerobic exercise that is involved can easily use the same number of calories as might be expended in a gym. Digging, raking, and mowing are particularly calorie intense; there is a gym outside many a window. The social interaction provided by communal and therapeutic garden projects for those with learning disabilities and poor mental health can counteract social isolation. Furthermore, it has also been reported that the social benefits of such projects can delay the symptoms of dementia (an effect that might be partly due to the beneficial effects of exercise). Patients who are recovering from myocardial infarction or stroke find that exercise in a garden, using constraint therapy of a paretic limb, for example, is more effective, enjoyable, and sustainable than therapy in formal exercise settings." (Retrieved from https://www.ncbi.nlm.nih.gov/pmc/articles/PMC6334070/)

If you live in an apartment, you can grow things in a sunny window. There is nothing quite like picking a tomato from your own plant and making a sandwich. No windows? Then get grow lamps and grow salads.

There is much good in gathering a bouquet of your own flowers to give to a neighbor. Gardening helps the environment; it helps your health. It makes you physically stronger. There are thousands of good books about gardening available from your public library. Gardening is one of those things that can be as inexpensive as a 99 cent package of seeds and a small sunny corner of your yard or as expensive as a full-out lawn tractor and everything in between. I find for most folks who have never gardened it's a good idea to start simply: if you have a yard, plant a few flowers, some annuals, and take care of them. If you don't have a yard, buy a tomato plant and a New Guinea Impatiens. Sit them in a sunny window and keep them watered twice a week; not sopping wet, but damp. They will bloom, flower, and the tomato will give you the reward of something to eat (as long as you remember to pollinate it) while the impatiens will reward you with flowers. If you have a patio or balcony outside your high rise, then set several pots of plants out there to take advantage of the fresh air. You'll enjoy puttering with them.

For those with houses that have lots, add some bright annual flowers to your yard along the edges; plant some perennials in places you know you'll want them to come up each year. There are many ways to get into gardening. I just know that the old poem

> "The kiss of the sun for pardon
> The song of the birds for mirth'
> I am nearer God's heart in my garden
> Than anywhere else on the earth."

has much truth in it.

Did you remember that He put our first parents in a garden to tend it? He had a reason. Gardening is good for us.

I will caution you again, though, not to start too large: I know one lady who decided, upon moving to a place with an already set up garden spot, that she was going to plant it up this year: and went to a gardening store, went a little nuts, and bought 29 packs of seeds she wanted to try! Unreal. Also really human -who can resist all those lovely pictures on the packets? Your garden can grow vegetables and help you budget or flowers to help your artistic side. Or both.

It's up to you. You're in control of what you grow. Know that there will be weeds to pull and watering to do when it's dry, but those are both good for you. You'll learn much from gardening. It's relaxing, it's enlightening and it's fun. And if you have kids, it's a grand family project. When they realize that what they grow they can eat, new ideas dawn in their brains.

I remember once I had a child staying with me for a while. I had been spading up potatoes that were ready for harvest. He was helping me pick them up. He got this funny expression on his face as I turned over the first hill.

"Mrs. Pelton, are these potatoes? Like in the store?"

I assured him these were indeed potatoes.

"You mean we're growing French fries?"

I told him yes, and mashed potatoes, boiled potatoes, creamed potatoes, hash browns . . . He went into a second or two of shock and then couldn't wait for me to turn over more potatoes. He'd had no idea they came from the ground.

When my kids were little, we had a garden with raised beds and I'd have each of them take a bed to tend. The garden was amazing; we ate fresh vegetables from it all summer, had flowers for fresh cut flowers all spring, summer, and into fall, and enjoyed the antics of groundhogs and other critters who came to join us in the beds.

Now that they're older, they all garden wherever they are living. One lives in a large city and has a small city lot but grows beautiful roses and herbs in back. Another lives with a large vegetable garden, still another has a small lot with flowers and succulents, vegetables and herbs. One lives in an apartment and grows just a few flowers along her walkway. They all grew up with a love of nature and a need to feel they are helping care for this old earth. It's not a bad thing to teach your children.

Art, music, gardening, to enrich your soul. Now, dust off your hands, put on your hat and pick up your walking stick. Time to leave this subject and move on down the hill to the final and perhaps most important thoughts on our trip.

Chapter Seven
A Day of Rest

I had a person tell me once that he wouldn't be so stressed if he had just a little more time to manage. He just couldn't seem to get everything done in a week. He worked Sunday through Thursday ten-hour shifts. By the time he got home, had some supper, read the paper, showered, checked his planner for tomorrow, it was bedtime. He told me in a very disgruntled way that he didn't even have time to watch TV. His schedule called for him to have Friday and Saturdays off, and most of the time he did unless the company called him in for a mandatory Friday. And on the time he had off, he had to do his shopping, mow the lawn, repair things around the house, fix the cars, change the oil; all you men know the drift of everyday life. His wife also worked 8 to 4: she dropped off the kids at school, put in a full day, came home to her latchkey kids, started her second shift of cleaning and laundry, cooking and helping with homework, taking care of the business of everyday life. He liked to watch a game in the afternoon on Saturday, but more likely than not, he'd watch it while working on the car in the garage. This couple was like hamsters on a wheel, working hard to go nowhere. He couldn't tell me when he last had time to play with his three kids. They were in school all day, Monday through Friday, and once home, they had homework, and they had supper, a couple of small chores, and then time to be tucked in. They each had one activity they had to go to each week – one had t-ball, one had dance classes, one was in softball. His wife carpooled with other equally busy wives to get the kids to the practice, the games, the occasional recital. Saturdays they saw Dad as they worked with him cleaning the yard or not at all. Kids saw Mom as the in-home pusher of homework and eating quickly so she could clean the kitchen or get whoever to their activity that night. They didn't know each other, and they all hated their life.

Mom was on Zoloft for anxiety, Dad was on Wellbutrin for depression, and the kids were heading for something.

Is this familiar? Are you running the same life they were? Has the recent forcing of yourself to stay home due to the virus woken you up to what you miss by allowing work to take your highest priority? Or do you feel shame at working at a "non-essential" job that you thought was essential until they told you it wasn't? Is your self-ego all tied up in your work? Perhaps you're in one of those essential positions and your life has only gotten more hectic. You have seriously missed the boat on life.

God knew when He created us that we'd have a tendency to run amuck. People who are under constant pressure to perform lose their capacity for good decision making. They get tension headaches; they develop high blood pressure. They make more errors; they allow short term choices to interfere with long term rewards. Somehow, their boss has taken control of them and they become, no matter how well-paid, wage slaves. Someone else owns their time and their priorities. Do you remember giving anyone that power? How did this happen to you?

Part of the original plan for stress and anxiety relief was to take one day in seven and rest. Way back at the time of creation, God set up one day in seven to stop everything and take time to simply rest, be together, not worry. No work, no interference, no interruptions.

No one owned that time. It belonged to family: God, His children, His creation. Let's take that apart for a moment before you tell me how impossible it is for you.

If you knew that each week, there was one day coming when you could sleep in a little later, no one had to go to work or to school, that you had the entire day together to do things you enjoyed; an entire day to worship, meditate, relax, and put aside everything and it was your choice to do so, what would you feel? Might make life pretty freeing, don't you think?

In the original plan, that is exactly what God had in mind. If you look back in Genesis to the written history of where it all began is written down, you will find that after God did all that creating in chapter 1 and 2, he set aside the seventh-day to sanctify it and make it holy. Here's how he put it in His words:

"Thus the heavens and the earth, and all the host of them, were finished. **2** And on the seventh day God ended His work which He had done, and He rested on the seventh day from all His work which He had done. **3** Then God blessed the seventh day and sanctified it, because in it He rested from all His work which God had created and made." Genesis 2:1-2

Now, being a therapist, I look at this a little bit differently than other people. I don't think God actually needed rest. I think he needed time to enjoy what he'd made. He had two new babies – Adam and Eve, and He just wanted a day to visit and talk and teach and finish falling in love with them. If

God, who runs the universe, wanted a day off each week, how can we feel that we don't need it? Are our families any less important than His?

I can attest to the truth that there is a satisfaction in getting everything in order each week on Friday, then enjoying what has been done on Sabbath. On our mini-farm, we walk around, see the progress on projects, see what's blooming, what's ready to be harvested, how the animals are doing, hold a barn kitten, visit with the grandkids – toss a football with one and an aerobie (flying ring) with another. I like to think of the first Sabbath in my mind's eye as a day God looked forward to each week, coming down from heaven and walking in the garden with Adam and Eve, just like today we spend time together as a family, eat a special meal, take a walk together and talk over the week and what were its ups and downs. Can you build a picture of Him showing Adam how to skip stones on the lake? Maybe showing Eve how to chain daisies for her head? The Sabbath of the Bible was instituted at the same time as marriage; He created Adam, then Eve, then married them and gave them the Sabbath to rest and get to know each other. Each week, they had the anniversary of the creation and of themselves and their love to grow closer. If you and your spouse have no time to get together, to talk, to rest and rejuvenate your love, then Sabbath is something your marriage direly needs to put into place.

Back in Eden, everything was marvelous before sin came in and it all fell apart and God had to write the other nine rules to keep our barbarian side in line. After creation, in the Bible story, there follows the sad history of the beginning of the Israelites and how they got put into slavery by the Egyptians.

God never intended for them to get in that fix either, but they did and since they did, by the time they got out of slavery (they were in Egypt 430 years!), they had unlearned the lessons about the Sabbath and the rest of the moral law; if someone else controls you, you'd don't get time off. Once they were out of Egypt, God reiterated to Moses the law, both ceremonial and moral.

The moral, eternal law, the Ten Commandments (which are still the basis for many of our own laws today), came first and right in the middle of them was the Sabbath, and it is the only commandment that begins with the world *Remember*. I suppose because we forget things that are good for us too easily.

Here's how God said it:

"Remember the Sabbath day, to keep it holy. **9** Six days you shall labor and do all your work, **10** but the seventh day *is* the Sabbath of the Lord your God. *In it* you shall do no work: you, nor your son, nor your daughter, nor your male servant, nor your female servant, nor your cattle, nor your stranger who *is* within your gates. **11** For *in* six days the Lord made the heavens and the earth, the sea, and all that *is* in them, and rested the seventh day. Therefore, the Lord blessed the Sabbath day and hallowed it." Exodus 20:8-11.

Now some folks have told me that all the other nine commandments – you know, thou shalt not kill, thou shalt not steal, thou shalt not commit adultery, are still valid but this one is not because it was "nailed to the cross" as being part of the ceremonial law and yet another person told me seriously it was for Jews only. Both ideas are a little bit disingenuous.

The Sabbath predated the other laws long before there was a Jewish nation. Jesus and the disciples before and after His death kept the Sabbath - that's historically documented. According to historians, it wasn't changed at all by God but by a man called Constantine of Rome, who wanted to unite his people around one day of worship and he chose the Venerable day of the Sun-the day they worshipped the sun-god – as the day of worship. Back in those days, around 300 A.D., you did what the state said or died. Churches went from being independent house churches to places where you met in special buildings, just like all the pagans, and the pagan Romans and Christians all got along. (Incidentally, Constantine exempted farmers from the new sabbath law, recognizing the need to care for farm animals.)

Here and there, small groups of people still worshipped on the Sabbath and they kept the knowledge of it and protected it.

In the meantime, people forgot all about the Sabbath and the reason for it and the human race became just that – a race to go faster, do faster, get more done, and we have been at it ever since, killing ourselves for no good reason.

It seems that as technology grows, our insistent demands that we get more done in less time just exist to make us more stressed. Stress pushes us and makes us irrational. It makes us worry and it makes us afraid. The strange thing is, we allow it. We give ourselves permission to work ourselves to death. We ignore our relationships, then wonder why our children don't love us and when they leave home, never seem to come back unless it's to ask for help. The last figures I saw were that 1 in 10 people in the U.S. were being treated for depression brought on by stress.

Do you remember family reunions? When I was a kid, we had a couple a year on the different sides of the family. I always liked the Augustine reunion held at Uncle Charlie's. Tons of food, lots of cousins to play with, and the pond we weren't supposed to go near, but somehow, someone always ended up falling into at some point. You don't hear much about family reunions anymore. We don't have time to get together anymore; we can't coordinate our own immediate family to get together for a meal around the table, much less the whole clan.

The Sabbath is a family reunion. You, your mate, your kids, and God get together. You forget about the mess outside and you concentrate on the love inside. It's a day of connections, a day you do random acts of kindness for neighbors.

During the time of the shelter in place, Sabbath is the time you all go out for that walk in the sunshine; it's the time you go out in the back yard or find a field and just talk. Take along a blanket to sit on and talk about the future, the things that matter, the places to go, what your plans are. Set aside the nagging nonsense that attacks during the week. Sabbath is the cure for not having time with your mate; it's time to focus on relationships.

Take along a book you've been reading to share some thoughts with the other person(s) in your family. If you are single, then this is a day to write letters, to send cards to neighbors. It is a day to completely do something different than usual.

In our family, we have always prepared for our Sabbath all week; when the kids were small, I or my husband planned outings to go on, places to walk, to visit. Since I have no small children at home now, it's a day my husband and I spend away from our businesses, we read, we visit by virtual community apps family in other cities; we ask our friends on social media what their prayer requests might be or what their real needs are right now, today. Sometimes it's something we can do; for instance, recently an older single lady was out of evaporated milk and we put together a little bag of things for her and hung it on her front door – she was watching and as soon as we were at the end of her drive, reached out and took it. We talk across the fence in back to our next-door lady and it keeps both our spirits up. I walk my dogs, check on my animals, and thank God he gave us a small place to care for and keep us occupied. Of late, I've set aside making quilts and have been making masks for folks I know who work in places that may not provide them. It's a day for giving to others.

"That's all very well right now when I'm at home and can't do anything else anyway," you are most likely saying. "Once this shelter at home stuff is over, I will be right back at work and I'll need to put in a lot of hours to make up for the unemployment which didn't come and the lack of income. My schedule will drop right back to where it was before. How is this Sabbath thing going to help me then?"

It helps by giving you space that's yours. It's not owned by anyone, it's time that's yours. No one orders you about; no social media or news programs; it's just you and those you love and God spending time, quality time, a whole day of time, doing what your mind and body need – resting.

It's not boring; sometimes I feel one-seventh of my time isn't enough to spend time doing the things I need to rejuvenate my soul. I have time to play and relax to good music; time to read a book I've been putting off, time to walk in the fresh air and admire those flowerbeds I spent all week working on, time to just sit and close my eyes and not have to worry about bells and driving through rush hour.

Lest you think it's simply a luxury you can't afford, you really can't afford *not* to do it. Research has shown that having time out from the work of life reduces stress and actually improves your productivity. It's like recovery time to an athlete; time spent rejuvenating your body so you can train harder when you return. Your brain is like a muscle; it needs rest, it grows when resting, it makes connections and works more creatively, more efficiently when you give it a rest. It's been found that people who take one day in seven off, even to the point of not getting on digital media or TV or anything else electronic, have clearer minds, clearer and stronger ability to make decisions. They also are not pushed around so easily; they have a source of hidden control.

"Just like **resting** physical muscles allows them opportunity to rejuvenate which leads to greater physical success, providing our minds with **rest** provides it opportunity to refocus and rejuvenate. More work is not better work. Smarter work is better work." (retrieved from https://www.becomingminimalist.com/resting/ April 18, 2020)

A rest day takes the focus off always getting, always working, and puts it back on what you have, what you are grateful for, who you love.

It's a time to refocus on what is truly important to you. The here and now can become too much a taskmaster, the taking on of constant projects prevents you building healthy relationships. You learn what is really important when you take time to think about life and you start to make changes.

You will find more contentment if you plan to rest and take rest each week. During the week, think ahead. Prepare a simple meal that takes no fussing to prepare and set it in the fridge. Plan the excursion you're going to take, either to walk your dog or yourself and family. Take along a camera and record sudden wonderful things. Expect to find good things and you will. Your attitudes will change; you are only as busy as you allow yourself to be. If you allow someone else to set your priorities, you have given them your life, and for what? Take the control back.

As you do, you will find that you will be braver, you will be stronger, you will have less anxiety because you refused to be pushed around by the job. Yes, you may love the job, but when you're old, what comfort will it be to look back and say, "wow, I was a really good (_____.) I should have spent more time doing that and less with my family." Will the job answer back and say yes, you were? If you've spent time with your family (of blood or of choice), building those relationships, they'll be there to answer you.

You need to embrace the simplicity that comes with having a day to yourself to reflect and relax and to worship. There is just one rule: avoid anything that seems like work unless it is to help someone else. For instance, one time we were walking in our neighborhood and a local older person was struggling to get their lawn mowed with a mower that he couldn't start. My husband took a moment, walked over, introduced himself as the guy from the white house with salamander green trim and the alpacas, and finagled a bit with the mower and got it going. Dan got it started, handed the man back his screwdriver and we continued on our way. It was a small lawn; he had it done before we got back around the block

124

and back, but he was very happy we'd helped. I suppose you could make the case that that was work, but to us, it was simply a RAK (Random Act of Kindness). Learning to live a life more simply by taking back one day a week away from work makes the other days of the week much more bearable.

Having a day to yourself and God helps you to live at peace and makes the acquisition of things less problematic. When you start enjoying what you have for one whole day, you would be astonished at how the world just goes on by itself, how it doesn't stop because you aren't killing yourself seven days a week. It puts a different perspective on what you do for the rest of the week. It makes you more efficient in that you plan for the rest day, so you prepare things ahead of time, you enjoy the rest day and at the end of it, you sleep better than before.

You actually get more done because you make better plans for what and how you're going to work later so you can do this again next week. Your kids will get used to having you play with them once a week; your spouse will love having your attention, and your soul turning to God and giving Him the day with you as it was in Eden will bring you a closeness spiritually you won't believe until you experience it. You can go to church in the morning or evening, you can worship at home with your loved ones, you can worship alone. Just turn off the phone, the distractions and spend time reading of Him and speaking to Him. It will rest you in ways you would not understand right now but will later.

For those who want to use them, I've written some short devotionals for you to use as you leave the path of fear and go on to the path of peace and strength. I've put them together in a small companion book to this one. In addition, I've also included a list of books to read that others have written in the appendix in case you should want to gather some up from the library or an online source to read and learn more about him. I am also including gardening books and other books that are useful. I do hope you will come and walk again with me on one of my mind journeys. I've put contact information in the back of the book if you should find a need to send me a message.

Until we meet again, may the good Lord bless and keep you and yours in the palm of His hand, and bless you as He sees you need.

A Final Word

Our journey has come to a close: if you have learned the principles of relaxation, and are using them, good. If you have found a way to be closer to yourself, your family and your God while relieving the stressors that threaten to engulf you, excellent. If you have just enjoyed the learning, that's good too.

Thank you so for reading this little book, written for the glory of God. I hope you will take the time to go to God, if you haven't already, and take advantage of His free gift. Your prayer does not have to be fancy. It can be something as simple as this:

Dear God, I know that I am a sinner and there is nothing that I can do to save myself. I confess my complete helplessness to forgive my own sin or to work my way to righteousness. At this moment I trust Christ alone as the One who bore my sin when He died on the cross. I believe that He did all that will ever be necessary for me to stand in your holy presence. Thank you for sending your Son to die in my place. I am grateful that He has promised to accept me just as I am right now. Father, I take you at your word. I believe you are my Lord and Creator and God. Thank you for the assurance that you will walk with me through all my life and even my death. Thank you for hearing this prayer and making me your child. Lead me in the way you would have me go from this time forward. In Jesus' Name. Amen.

If you pray this prayer, or one like it, please contact me and let me know. I'd love to send you some information to help you on your new life path.

My webpage address is:

Travelerpelton.com

My facebook is travelerpelton

While you're there, I hope you take the time to get acquainted with us, the writers at Potpourri Publishing – because now we are members of the family of God, and I'd love to meet you!

And remember my invitation; when we get to heaven, at that last day, you'll find the tree of life spanning the river of life. The first Sabbath, I will be with Jesus and the Father and my angel celebrating my first Sabbath in heaven. The second Sabbath, I will be with my family, all the generations back to Adam, again, celebrating. But that next Sabbath is for all of us, my friends, my fans, the people I have learned to love over the years spent here on earth. On the third Sabbath after we get there, we're all meeting on the left bank for a potluck and to share our stories. We'd be pleased if you'd join us there. It's going to be grand! I can't wait to meet all of you. May God bless.

Promised Book Suggestions to continue your walk...

I promised you a list of books I have found useful in my own walk with God. I am quite eclectic: I read from authors of all faith persuasions for I feel we can all learn from each other. I am a practicing Seventh-day Adventist; that does not keep me from reading and absorbing the good in others. Here are some books you may find helpful:

First of all, and foremost is the Bible. I enjoy the Peshitta translation by Lamsa, The New King James, and once in a while one of the modern paraphrases. I found reading the Chronological Bible fascinating, as it puts it all in historical order, instead of its usual order and it fixes better in your mind just what periods things occurred. Whichever is your favorite, reading it each day is important. Start in one of the gospels if you are new to it, I would suggest Luke, and read each day until you have learned something new. I don't know how many times I have gone through the Bible: I've been reading it since I was 12 or 14 and got the first one that was mine completely. I always see something new each time.

Other books of interest:

By Max Lucado

- Six Hours One Friday,
- When God Whispers Your Name
- 3:16 The Numbers of Hope
- Unshakable Hope

By Philip Yancy

- The Jesus I Never Knew
- <u>What's So Amazing About Grace?</u>
- <u>Where Is God When It Hurts?</u>

By Morris Venden

- Obedience by Faith
- Love God and Do as You Please
- Modern Parables
- Your Friend, The Holy Spirit
- 95 Thesis on Righteousness' by Faith

Clifford Goldstein

- Life Without Limits

CS Lewis

- The Screwtape Letters
- Mere Christianity
- The Problem of Pain
- (And for fun) The Chronicles of Narnia

Chuck Swindoll

- Improving Your Serve
- Growing Strong in the Seasons of Life
- Living Beyond the Daily Grind

Lee Strobel

- The Case for Christ

Ellen G. White

- Steps to Christ

- Christ's Object Lessons
- The Sanctified Life

Francis Schaeffer

- How Then Should We Live?
- A Christian Manifesto

Philip Keller

- A Shepherd Looks at Psalm 23
- Sky Edge
- Sea Edge
- Lessons from a Sheep Dog

Johnathan Cahn

- The Harbinger
- The Mystery of Shemitah
- The Paradigm

Gardening Books

- Vegetable Gardening for Beginners: A Simple Guide to Growing Vegetables at Home by Jill McSheehy
- Mini Farming: Self-Sufficiency on 1/4 Acre by Brett L. Markham
- Raised Bed Gardening: How to Start and Sustain a Garden with Less Space Even if You Are a Beginner. Build a Thriving Organic System in an Urban Setting ... (Hydroponics & Greenhouse Gardening Book 5) by John Crops and Urban Homesteading School
- All New Square Foot Gardening, 3rd Edition, Fully Updated:• MORE Projects • NEW Solutions • GROW Vegetables Anywhere by Mel

Bartholomew (this was my first gardening book in my library and I still refer to it!)
- How Not to Kill Your Houseplant: Survival Tips for the Horticulturally Challenged by Veronica Peerless
- Urban Gardening for Beginners: Simple Hacks and Easy Projects for Growing Your Own Food in Small Spaces by Marc Thoma

Books about Art and Music of Interest

- This Is Your Brain on Music: The Science of a Human Obsession by Daniel J. Levitin
- The Body Keeps the Score: Brain, Mind, and Body in the Healing of Trauma by Bessel Van der Kolk MD, Sean Pratt, et al.
- Musicophilia by Oliver Sacks
- The Anxiety Journal: Exercises to Soothe Stress and Eliminate Anxiety Wherever You Are : A Guided Journal by Corinne Sweet

And I would be honored if you would consider my own books, which I have listed at the beginning of this book as reading you might also enjoy.

As an example of some of the devotionals in the little companion book, I am enclosing a couple for you to use in your own quiet time:

Day 1

Fear not, for I *am* with you; Be not dismayed, for I *am* your God. I will strengthen you, Yes, I will help you, I will uphold you with My righteous right hand. Isaiah 41:10

Let me say this upfront; fear is a normal emotion. It is a simply biochemical reaction to danger. Being afraid does not have to be the end of things, it can simply be there to let you know what to do next.

I remember as a child my dad bought 28 acres of land in West Virginia, what he actually bought was his own small mountain, or at least most of one side of it. We were walking along the path around it up to the peak where sat some huge boulders, flattened from being on top a mountain. It was a shady walk, a hot day and we were, my sister Cindy and I, just taking our time. Dad and Mom were about fifty feet behind us. Dad was explaining to Mom that there was a real nice spot for a cabin up ahead, could see over the whole countryside from that place. He also mentioned he got mineral rights and they'd have a small check coming in from the oil company every quarter. They weren't paying too much attention to us as we ambled along.

Suddenly Cindy froze in her tracks and started to shake. I looked ahead of her and gave a yelp of surprise. There, in the road about twelve feet in front of us, in a sunny spot lay about the largest snake I'd ever seen. It was just lying there, enjoying the sin and it hadn't noticed us. I started to back up, really slowly. Cindy froze. I called back to Dad.

"Daddy there's an awful big snake up here."

I can still hear Dad's exclamation. He ran up, grabbed up Cindy and told me to get back to Mom. It turned out to be a copperhead, something Dad, who grew up in West Virginia, was acquainted with and I, growing up until then in Ohio, was not. He got us back far enough, then Dad picked up several large rocks and commenced throwing them at the snake, who slithered off.

Mom was too shaken up to continue the walk up the hill that morning. They walked up later that day but without the kids and with Dad carrying a sharpened hoe unless that beast had come back.

Yes, I was afraid, so was Cindy, so was Dad. But the difference was, we did something about the fear. We got away from the danger. In life, there are dangers, real dangers to be worried about. False dangers, things that might happen or could happen or possibly happen, are nothing to worry about. Be content and deal with the real dangers. God tells us He will always be with us, not to dismayed, or frightened. He is there to keep us and help us decide what is the right route to go. Don't lose sleep over what might never happen.

Dad never did build that cabin. Mom decided that Ohio was a safer place to raise kids because the worst snake she'd ever seen here was a garden snake.

"Fear is your friend. It is an indicator. Sometimes it shows you what you shouldn't do, more often than not it

shows you what you should do." *Tim Ferriss*

Day Two

Peace I leave with you; my peace I give you. I do not give to you as the world gives. Do not let your hearts be troubled and do not be afraid. John 14:27

The peace God is speaking of here is the peace a child feels as they snuggle in their parent's arms, no matter what is happening around them.

I remember a story my dad told me when I was a child, something he had witnessed that had stuck with him until he died an old man.

He was in World War II. He was in the Air Force and he traveled all over the world doing maintenance and fueling the plane for the actual pilots. He had always wanted to be a pilot, but he was nearsighted and back then you couldn't fly with glasses. He contented himself with being the man on the ground backing them up.

He went to China, India, and England among other places. He told me the story of how at one place, they were seeing heavy action. They had native people do housekeeping chores for them on the base and during the fighting, he'd fuel a plane, lock it down as he called it, jump down and the plane would rumble out, another take it's place and he'd fill that one.

During a lull, they'd run back into the tent barracks and grab some coffee or relieve themselves. On his trip to the latrine, he saw several of the housekeepers hiding behind the latrines, holding their children in their arms. He didn't speak the language and he asked what on earth they were back there for from someone who did.

"They say they never bomb latrines. They bomb weapons and planes and barracks, they not bomb toilets. Safest place to be." He was told. He shook his head and went back to work.

The thing that struck him though was that all four women had babies in their arms who were sleeping through the entire bombing. It was as if a war was not going on. They were in their mother's arms and as far as the babies were concerned, they were safe. He said he never lost the picture of those ladies behind the bathrooms, holding sleeping babies while the sound of war all around them went on. The world might be crazy but the babies had peace.

Was it a peace that the world gives? Heavens no! It's the kind of peace we can feel inside us when everything around us is falling into small pieces. So, are we surrounded by invisible viruses and we have to hunker down in our homes, not go out except for emergencies and provisions, not see anyone? That's fine. Be glad there is a home to hunker down in. Be glad there is food. Be glad you are safe in your home. Be thankful that there are folks out there fighting the virus. And look forward to the flowers of spring and summer, and the thought that this too shall pass and know that there is nothing to fear.

Take care of those you love, take comfort in them and have confidence in Him. If you are alone, or feel alone, take comfort that you are not really alone, for there is One over all who watches and hears you. If you are a single person and have no one to speak with, speak with Him. He's a great listener. Find ways to do kindnesses for others. The anticipation of doing something for someone else, even if it's to bake a good loaf of bread and give it to a neighbor, or make masks to donate at the local fire department, or just writing a letter to someone who's as housebound as yourself – all of those can ease the loneliness. Relax into your Father's love.

"Never be in a hurry; do everything quietly and in a calm spirit. Do not lose your inner peace for anything whatsoever, even if your whole world seems upset." Saint Francis de Sales

If you enjoy Christian fiction, you might enjoy the series I completed last year called The Oberllyn Family Chronicles. It traces the stories of a single family through three centuries in America, past, present times, and future, with an eye on warning all those of us who love liberty and love the Lord what could happen to our freedoms if we don't guard them and pay attention to what is happening. The first book in the Series, The Oberllyn's Overland, deals with the family at the time of the Civil war. *Here's the first chapter:*

"Well, mother, it's just about all I can stand," remarked Elijah Oberllyn as he stepped into the kitchen.

"What happened this time?" answered his wife Elizabeth. She was busy rolling out the dough for homemade noodles on the wooden kitchen table. Behind her on the woodstove was bubbling a rich broth to cook them in. From the oven came the wonderful smell of peach pie baking, and warm bread stood on the counter, covered in tea towels. Elizabeth was short woman, with her long black hair, just starting to show grey, done up in a bun at the back of her neck, wearing a solid brown apron over a calico brown dress, and she looked capable of taking on the entire army and feeding it at once. Bustling as she rolled out the dough, she reminded you of a wren on a branch, swaying and hopping from task to task, chirping merrily in between.

"That neighbor Jacks," began her husband. "He's let his cattle get into my wheat again. He says he'll mend the fence but this time he said it was my fault because if I hadn't planted wheat, his cows wouldn't have been tempted, and he is talking about suing me for tempting his cows!"

His wife looked at him and finally said, "You're serious? He is going to try suing you for tempting cows?" She started to laugh out loud but hushed herself when she saw how angry her husband was. "It appears to me the only person to benefit from that would be the lawyers."

"He wants my field to add to his farm. He won't mend the fences on purpose. He's expecting me to do his fence. He's doing the same thing to our son. He offered him a pittance for his orchard, and when Noah wouldn't sell, he started rumors about him being half crazed since the church kicked him out during the great Disappointment and not being right so some of our own neighbors are questioning us for having our own services and I simply am not sure what to do. It's bad enough he picks on us but really, taking off after my son is just about all I can stand." Elizabeth considered for a moment, then said quietly to her husband,

"It's not much of a witness to be fighting with the neighbors. Joe wants to go to California to hunt for gold, but Catherine is not about to drop everything for a wild goose chase. Noah seems content here. I haven't spoken to Mary or Emily about it. I suppose we could consider moving but I hate the idea."

"We've lived here peaceably with our neighbors for years. It's only since those Jacks moved into their uncle's farm we've had trouble. Our land is fertile enough, but when Jacks heard we'd tried to buy his uncle's farm once, he took a dislike to us. And now look." Her husband poured himself a cup of coffee and sat down, blowing on it to cool it, then looking at is wife with a pensive expression on his face.

"California is a right far piece to go," he started.

"Elijah! I was only giving you ideas from different members of the family, not saying I wanted to go." His wife turned with her hands on her hips, a distinctly displeased look on her face.

"It's a good idea and I might have to look into it. I don't want to be run out of town on a rail and that's just what that Jack's fellow is going to try and make happen. Besides, it's getting too crowded around here. It wasn't so bad before that train got put in. Now there are more people coming to buy land and settle in and it's just too crowded."

"Well, you need to pray about anything before you go off half-cocked," she said firmly. "Now go do your chores whilst I finish up supper."

Elijah went back to his barn and finished cleaning out stalls. His wife's jerseys would be up soon for milking. They'd cost him a pretty penny when he'd gotten them, but had proven to be just what Ma's dairy business needed. They gave rich milk, it made wonderful cheese and butter, and their farm was getting known for its good fruit and cheese. Until that neighbor had moved here, everything had been going along fine. Joe had a good thought, though. Out west, there was plenty of land and it wasn't crowded. They could worship as they pleased on Saturday and not be accused of being Judaizers or crazy or anything else. He had two more children at home and there'd be no land to give them as a farm of their own if he couldn't buy up some land. When his son Nathaniel got married, it was a good thing he was a doctor who hadn't time to farm. The farm was just too divided up as it was, what with Emily and her brood, and Catherine and David over by the creek running the small fruits part of the family business. Miriam's man Joe being a lawyer had helped; they'd just needed land for a house and little garden for themselves, no real farming involved. Noah and Mary had taken over the fruit orchard and were making a good go of it, and he and Elizabeth still had enough for him to raise the best horses and oxen in the county and keep mom's dairy running, but they needed more land. It just couldn't be divided anymore and there was Thomas and Johanna yet to be grown and have a part. He supposed Thomas could inherit their home but where would Joanna go? And that Jacks trying to force them to sell land to him they didn't have to spare, he and his dirty tricks. Hard to imagine what he'd try next. Maybe Joe had a good idea. *I believe I'll just visit the land office and find out about land west of here. It surely wouldn't be bad to have a look.*

He came out of the barn and stretched. His son Thomas came dashing up; that child never went anywhere at a walk, always running. "Pa, you got a letter."

"Oh? Thank you, son. Let's have a look." He took the letter from him. It was an official looking document from the US government.

"Haven't seen one of these since well before you were born."

"Was that back when you and mama lived in New York?"

"Yes, pretty much when you were a baby, before grandpa died and we inherited the farm."

"Wonder what they want?"

"Whatever it is, your mom and I will deal with it. You're supposed to have seen to the goats."

"Done. You know the mom angora is going to give birth any day?" he grinned. "Can't wait to see them. I love the way the babies sprong around."

"Well, you keep a good eye on her."

Thomas hesitated. "Pa, I saw Mike Jacks over looking at mom's sheep. He had this funny look on his face?"

"Funny like how?"

"He said his dad doesn't like sheep, they ruin the field. I told him it wasn't his field so not to worry about it. He said something under his breath and walked off. I don't like him much, pa. I was hoping for a friend that would move in that I could do stuff with but I don't think he likes me much."

"Don't worry about him. There are other folks to be with that don't cause such aggravation. Just be civil and leave him be."

"Yes, Pa. He made Johanna cry. Oh!" he covered his mouth.

"What?"

"I wasn't supposed to tell you."

"Stop right now. You don't keep secrets from me, ever. When was Johanna crying?"

"She went out to get the cows yesterday and Ellie Jacks was waiting and called her a cowgirl and teased her about her hair."

"What's wrong with her hair?"

"It's sort of red, I guess. And Johanna was crying when she helped with milking."

"I see. And you weren't supposed to tell me?"

"Johanna said we were having enough trouble with this family and God wouldn't want her complaining about it."

"I see. Well, you just let me handle this. Must be about time for supper, yes, there's mom ringing the dinner bell. Let's go wash up."

Dad and Thomas washed up at the pump and went inside, hanging their hats by the door.

"That smell sure chirks a fellow up, Ma. Can't wait to have some of your chicken and noodles."

Elizabeth smiled. "Johanna, would you mind getting the field tea I made? I put it in the springhouse to get cold."

Johanna nodded and went out the door, coming back with a pitcher covered in a towel. "Mom," she frowned. "I don't think we ought to use the tea."

"What's the matter?"

"Somebody's been in the spring house."

"Really? How do you know?"

"The cheeses are all on the floor and the milk's spilt."
Ma and Pa rushed outside to the spring house where they found rounds of cheese scattered all over, the five-gallon milk cans flipped, polluting the spring run over. They looked around at the damage. Ma shook her head.

"I hate to think we'd have to put guards on our home, but this is outrageous."

"If we tell the sheriff," began Thomas.

"He'll say it could've been done by animals, that someone left the door open. There's no proof."

"Why don't we make a list of what's going on at least and ask him to watch out with us?" asked Ma.

"We can do that. Are the cheeses ruined?"

"The shelves are broken down, but the cheese ought to be fine. I may have to rewrap some."

"Let's see what we can do. Thomas – call Mick and Mike." Mike and Mick were the family mastiffs who spent most the time in the back field with the cattle. The dogs came to Thomas's call. "We'd best keep the dogs close to the yard or at least one of them here."

"Then who's going to protect the cattle from coyotes?" asked Thomas.

"It's not the four-legged ones I am worried about just now."

Thomas and Dad reset the shelves and they helped Mom wipe off the wax coated cheeses and set them back. While they did that, Mom set the milk cans up and opened the overflow wide so the water could drain out and run clear. Finally, they stood up and went out. Dad shut the door to the spring house and set Mike by the door, telling him to stay. He took Mick to the barn and set him there and they went inside to eat.

The meal was a quiet one. Ma and Pa were tight-lipped, and Thomas and Johanna were quiet as they passed food around.

"I don't care what they say. Johanna, you have got the prettiest hair in the world. It shines in the sun like gold and when you wear your green Sabbath dress, I have the prettiest sister in the county."

Johanna looked surprised and her eyes welled up. "Thank you," she whispered.

"I agree with your brother. I am not quite sure why he said it but thank you for noticing," said Pa. Mom and Johanna just looked confused. Suddenly, there was a loud meow from out back.

"What on earth!" said Ma, getting up. She went out back where a strange collie dog had her pet cat up a tree. She took a switch and chased it off. The dog ran to the end of the driveway where Mike Jacks was watching.

"Lady, you'd better not hurt my dog," he yelled at her.

"Then keep him on your own land," she replied.

"Well, this is going to be our land when my dad gets done with you," he yelled back. "You'd better not let those sheep overgraze it." Mom picked up a bigger switch and headed down the drive purposefully in his direction and he ran off. A passing wagon stopped.

"You all right, Mrs. Oberllyn?" said the farmer driving.

"I don't know, Zeb. We got neighbor problems. My spring house was attacked, they insult us, and we just never did them any harm."

"I heard about some of that. Mr. Jacks was in the general store last week boasting he'd have your land soon. I don't know what he was talking about, but I was coming to tell your husband if he was going to sell out, to call on me. I could use good fields like yours."

"I thank you, and I'll tell Elijah, but we have no interest in leaving our farm. It's been in the family for over a hundred years."

"Thought he might be blowing smoke. But still, keep me and my sons in mind. I'd rather buy from you than Jacks. Oh, and best be careful. There's some weird rumors going around." Elijah was on the porch and waved to his neighbor.

"Rumors?"

"I'm sure they ain't true. You say howdy to Elijah for me."

"Thank you, Zeb. By the way, did he happen to say why he wanted my land?"

"He said it was the best land in the district and I have to agree with him. Your orchards make the best fruit, your cheese is wonderful, and you've always been real supportive of our community. Shame to have you leave."

"Aren't planning on leaving."

"I hope not. Well, I best be getting home. You remember my offer."

Mom went to the back where Thomas had climbed the tree and gotten her Maine coon cat down. He jumped into her arms. "There, there, dear. I'm sorry he flustered you so. Shh, now. Shhh."

"Mom, why do they hate us?"

"I have no idea." They went inside. "We've never had this much trouble."

"Mom, did you know Jacks have got slaves?"

"What?"

"They have three of them. I saw them out working his field. And Mr. Jacks carries a whip."

"I see. Well, the good Lord never wanted slavery. We earn our needs by the works of our hands, not the sweat of others. Let's try to finish supper. It's most likely all cold by now."

About the Author:

J. Traveler Pelton was born in West Virginia in the last century. She served as Nation's Mother for her tribe for six years. She is wife to Dan (46 years!), mother of six adults, a grandmother of eight, a Clinically Licensed Independent Social Worker with Supervisory Status, at present in private practice, a retired adjunct professor of social work at her local university and an insatiable reader. She is a cancer survivor. Traveler avidly studies science and technology, fascinated by the inventiveness of people. She is quick to draw parallels in different fields and weave stories around them. Traveler is a fabric artist and her most enjoyable time is spent spinning yarn while spinning yarns for the grandkids.

You can reach Traveler at her website:

travelerpelton.com

Or like us and share us on **Facebook at Traveler Pelton**

Or write to her by **snail mail** at

Springhaven Croft
216 Sychar Rd.
Mt. Vernon, OH 43050
She loves to hear from her readers!
All our books are available on Amazon as both eBook and print copy, Kindle unlimited as free downloads

We'd love it if you'd leave us a review! It helps others find our books.

God bless and see you in our next travels together!

Your Attention Please!!!!

Would you like to join the team at Potpourri Books?

Traveler is <u>always</u> looking for responsible beta readers for her new books. A beta reader gets a prepublication copy of all new books, <u>free of charge</u> in exchange for an honest review written on Amazon, and a short email letting her know of any glitches you may have found that got past the editor, any suggestions you may have, and your opinion of the book. What else do you get out of it?

A beta reader gets:

A free download of one of her already published books and

as soon as your review of that book gets placed on Amazon,

free downloads of her already published works: for each review, you get a free book.

And

A free copy pre publication copy of all new books…

And

Other neat freebies as they come, from bookmarks to stickers to posters to pens to neat things I find to send out to my betas-

Interested?

Contact Traveler at

travelerpelton@gmail.com for more info…

We would love to add you to the team!

Blessings for you:

Dear Lord,
Give me a few friends
who will love me for what I am,
and keep ever burning
before my vagrant steps
the kindly light of hope...
And though I come not within sight
of the castle of my dreams,
teach me to be thankful for life,
and for time's olden memories
that are good and sweet.
And may the evening's twilight
find me gentle still.

Old Celtic blessing....

I've seen better days, but I've also seen worse.

I don't have everything that I want, but I do have all I need.

I woke up with some aches and pains, but I woke up.

My life may not be perfect, but I am blessed."

Anonymous

Until you join me on another journey, may you be blessed as well!

Made in the USA
Monee, IL
05 August 2020